The Golden Thread

Other Books by Ken R. Vincent

Visions of God from the Near-Death Experience (1994)

The Magi: From Zoroaster to the "Three Wise Men" (1999)

The Golden Thread

◆

God's Promise of Universal Salvation

Ken R. Vincent

iUniverse, Inc.
New York Lincoln Shanghai

The Golden Thread
God's Promise of Universal Salvation

Copyright © 2005 by Ken R. Vincent

All rights reserved. No part of this book may be used or reproduced by any means, graphic, electronic, or mechanical, including photocopying, recording, taping or by any information storage retrieval system without the written permission of the publisher except in the case of brief quotations embodied in critical articles and reviews.

iUniverse books may be ordered through booksellers or by contacting:

iUniverse
2021 Pine Lake Road, Suite 100
Lincoln, NE 68512
www.iuniverse.com
1-800-Authors (1-800-288-4677)

ISBN-13: 978-0-595-36683-5 (pbk)
ISBN-13: 978-0-595-81105-2 (ebk)
ISBN-10: 0-595-36683-X (pbk)
ISBN-10: 0-595-81105-1 (ebk)

Printed in the United States of America

Contents

Permissions ix
Prologue 1
CHAPTER 1   What Is Universal Restoration? 3
CHAPTER 2   God's Promise of Universal Salvation in the Hebrew Scriptures 8
CHAPTER 3   God's Promise of Forgiveness in the Hebrew Scriptures 13
CHAPTER 4   Judgment According to the New Testament 18
CHAPTER 5   Hell Is for Rehabilitation 24
CHAPTER 6   Universal Salvation According to the New Testament 28
CHAPTER 7   Mystical Religious Experiences and Christian Universalism 39
CHAPTER 8   The Near-Death Experience and Christian Universalism 53
CHAPTER 9   "All Flesh Shall See the Salvation of God" 67
Epilogue 75

Appendices

APPENDIX A   New Testament Verses Supporting Salvation by Works 83

Appendix B	New Testament Verses Supporting Universal Salvation 85
Appendix C	Old Testament (Hebrew Bible) Verses Supporting Universal Salvation. 87
Appendix D	Funeral Service Stressing Universal Salvation 89
Appendix E	Funeral Service for a Beloved Pet 93
Appendix F	Funeral Service for a Non-Christian in a Christian Family 95
Appendix G	Christian Universalism "Endorsed" by Jesus Seminar 97
Appendix H	Magic, Deeds, and Universalism 101

Notes. 107

Primary Sources. 109

References 113

Acknowledgment

This book is a reality because of the help and support of my wife Pam.

Permissions

Scriptures quoted from *The Holy Bible, New Century Version (NCV)*, copyright © 1987, 1988, 1991, by Word Publishing, Dallas, Texas 75234. Used by permission.

The Scripture quotations contained herein from the *New Revised Standard Version Bible (NRSV)*, copyright © 1989 by the Division of Christian Education of the National Council of the Churches of Christ in the U.S.A. Used by permission. All rights reserved.

Chapter 8, "The Near-Death Experience and Christian Universalism" is based on an article by the same name that appeared in the *Journal of Near-Death Studies,* 22 (1), Fall 2003, 57-71 Used by permission of IANDS.

Appendix G, "Christian Universalism 'Endorsed' by the Jesus Seminar" and *Appendix H*, "Magic, Deeds, and Universalism" were first published in the *Universalist Herald* which was given first North American Serial Rights.

Prologue

My parents were good Methodists who made sure that I attended Sunday school faithfully. Learning about Jesus and his Sermon on the Mount made a lasting impression on me! In a very real way, this book represents the culmination of a lifetime of love for Jesus' teachings, as well as recognition of the special friends who have enriched my religious journey.

In the America of my childhood, ordinary people did not spend much time thinking about religious diversity. For the most part, people were either Christians who attended church or Christians who stayed home on Sundays. It would be safe to say that most of my fellow Americans from the pre-"baby-boomer" generation would not have personally known anyone who wasn't Christian. This was true not only for the "Bible Belt" but also throughout America's heartland and across the states from coast to coast.

Thankfully, I had the good fortune to have three childhood friends who were Jewish. (Later I learned that many Jews during that era chose to remain "invisible" due to cultural discrimination.) I was sure that my Jewish buddies were as good as any Christians I knew, and I was bothered when many adults told me that these non-Christian friends were destined for Hell! To me, this possibility seemed contrary to Jesus' admonition to not only *be* good but to *do* good and his teaching that all the people of the world were judged on the basis of their good works (Matthew 25:31-46). My parents assured me that my Jewish friends would go to Heaven, but other relatives said, well—they hoped so! Only my Great Aunt Alice offered what seemed to me to be the best possible scenario. She was a Universalist, and she was positive that *all* people went to Heaven! When I asked her where that was found in the *Bible*, she could only say confidently, "It's in there!" Aunt Alice was not a *Bible* scholar, but her certitude inspired me to produce a source where you, the reader, can easily discover the *Golden Thread* of Universal Salvation that weaves its way through both the *Hebrew Bible (Old Testament)* and the *New Testament*.

With the passing of just half a century, the populace of contemporary America presents a stark contrast to the one of my youth. To its credit, our nation has discarded a lot of racial and religious discrimination and hypocrisy, and our society has been greatly enriched by a growing religious and ethnic diversity. In today's multi-cultural America, my valued friends represent a tapestry of world religions I scarcely knew existed when I was a child—Zoroastrianism, Taoism, Sikhism, Islam, Hinduism, and Buddhism. In our ordinary, everyday work, school, or social activities, it is no longer unusual to be acquainted with genuinely good people, including many exemplary human beings, who are devoted followers of all these religions. More importantly, these inter-religious friendships highlight the urgent need for today's world to hear the *Bible*'s ancient Universalist message that reminds all who share this globe of a God who promises salvation for *all*.

Unfortunately, too many Christians still cling to a view of God that is restricted and exclusive. They overlook the *Golden Thread* of Universalist theology found throughout the *Bible* declaring that God is the God of us *all*. Over and over, the *Bible* tells of a God who is not just Savior of the few but a Universal God who is Savior of *all*—the God Jesus talked about! Jesus taught that we are to love one another, that God's love is unconditional, and that in the end, God will save the "Lost Sheep" and the "Prodigal Son."

Universal Restoration has been an ongoing passion of mine for virtually all my adult life. In researching this book, I have incorporated the thinking of Universalist scholars from earliest Christianity to the present. As you read through these *Bible* verses, mystical religious experiences, and near-death experiences, I hope that you will find comfort in the message of a loving God who is too good to condemn any of us to Eternal Hell. I am confident that you will discover joy in the *Golden Thread* of Universalism that is God's promise to us *all*.

1

What Is Universal Restoration?

Do you believe that people who are not Christian go to Heaven? If you have found it difficult to believe that a loving God would condemn non-Christians to Eternal Hell, then you will be interested in learning more about Universalism. Salvation for *all* is known as Universalism, and the idea that *all* people will be saved—either immediately or eventually—is called Universal Restoration. This is not some New Age idea but an ancient truth that weaves its way like a *Golden Thread* throughout the same *Holy Bible* you have known since childhood! It has been embraced by Christians from the early Jesus Movement to modern Biblical scholars. Although some ministers seem reluctant to discard their threats of a terrifying, vengeful God, this book offers proof that the *Bible* is equally strewn with verses that describe a loving God, the good parent who desires that *all* of us be saved.

In compiling this book, my goal was to put the *Bible* verses supporting Universalist theology in an easily accessible format and let the evidence speak for itself. Writings of the great liberal thinkers from Origen in the 3rd century to John Hick in the 21st Century were consulted.

Universalist Theology

The first major Universalist Christian theologian whose work survives is Origen (185-254 CE). He adopted a doctrine of Universal Restoration, the idea that all who do good works go to Heaven, and that *all* people will be saved either immediately or eventually. The validity of this view is based on the *New Testament* itself which contains more verses that advocate Universal Restoration than verses which prescribe "belief in Jesus" as the singular gateway to God. Sadly, the prominent role given by the *New Testament* writers to the loving message of Universalism is rarely heard in modern pulpits.

Conservative Christians often use one verse from the Gospel of John as the cornerstone of their theology: **"I am the way, and the truth, and the life. No** one comes to the Father except through me" (Jn 14:6). Universalist Christian theologians like Tom Harpur (Anglican) and John Hick (United Reformed Church) interpret this passage to mean that salvation comes by following the teachings of Jesus rather than from adherence to some formula of belief. In other words, Jesus brought us the Word (Jn 1:14). "Belief in Jesus" brings salvation *only* if it inspires the believer to *do good deeds*!

Good Works

Jesus emphasizes that empty words of commitment won't suffice and that salvation belongs to those who do God's will (Matt 7:21). Unlike theology that rests on very few verses, the verses that advocate Salvation by Good Works dominate all others in the *New Testament* with the majority of verses supporting it on the lips of Jesus himself! Jesus tells us, **"Let your light shine before others, so that they may see your good works and give glory to your Father in heaven"** (Matt 5:16). Christians need to remember that their efforts to make the world better all flow from Jesus' great mandate to do good to others in "The Judgment of the Nations" (Matt 25: 31-46). This message is heard in the text of Charles Dickens' *A Christmas Carol*, in Louisa May Alcott's *Little Women*, and in Henry Van Dyke's *The Story of the Other Wise Man*. More importantly, it is reflected in the values of Clara Barton, Florence Nightingale, Mother Teresa, St. Francis, Thomas Jefferson, Abraham Lincoln, Gandhi, Martin Luther King, and Nelson Mandella.

Over two hundred years ago, the Universalist John Murry wrote: "You may possess only a small light but uncover it, let it shine, use it in order to bring more light and understanding to the hearts and minds of men and women. Give them, not Hell, but hope and courage. Do not push them deeper into their theological despair, but preach the kindness and everlasting love of God."

I think that the most important of Jesus' teachings about our own behavior is one unique to him: **"Do not judge, and you will not be judged"** (Lk 6:37). Since our own judgment is dependent on the compassion we show to others, everyone benefits when we stop and think before we speak. Jesus did not expect people to be perfect, but he did teach them how to become the best they can be. He said that God is our parent (Matt 6:9, 23:9) and that we could trust that, **"for God all things are possible"** (Matt: 19:26).

Universal Salvation

Second only to the number of *Bible* verses supporting Good Works are those verses supporting the theology of eventual Universal Salvation. The two taken together (Good Works + Universal Salvation) form the case for Universal Restoration.

When the chief priests and the elders question Jesus' authority, he declares that, **"tax collectors and prostitutes are going to the kingdom of God ahead of you"** (Matt 21:31). The key word in Jesus' statement is "ahead." He asserts that *all* will reach the Kingdom but that even sexual deviants and agents of the oppressive foreign government will enter before the hypocritical orthodox priests!

The *Bible* also talks about God's grace and the promise of Universal Salvation (Jn 12:32, Eph 1:9-10). God's loving presence is more powerful than we can imagine. The *Bible's* message is that God is always present (Eph 4:6) and that God's love for us is unconditional (Lam 3:22). Universal Restoration combines our own good works and the universal grace of God. In the end, we are promised that "all flesh shall see the Salvation of God" (Lk 3:6).

The idea of Universal Salvation has several permutations within the *Bible*, but the end result of each is the same. For some, Universal Restoration is the result of God's eternal grace, and Jesus is the teacher who shows us the Way (1 Tim 2:3-5). For others, Universal Salvation comes through Jesus' symbolic sacrifice (1 Cor 15:21-28).

Universalism As A Denomination

In the 18th Century, the American Universalist Church was established upon the tenant that God was too good to damn people to Eternal Hell. This idea became so popular during the 19th Century that the denomination grew to be the 6th largest in the United States; however, its decline is often blamed on its success. Eventually, the appeal of this benign message motivated mainline churches of the time to de-emphasize their less-than-loving messages of hellfire and predestination, and there was less incentive for people to change denominations. Today, a remnant of the Universalist Church of America survives within the interfaith Unitarian Universalist Association. However, Christians who advocate Universal Restoration can be found in virtually all denominations from post-Vatican II Catholics to Primitive Baptists. Universalism is a way of understanding God's love as revealed through the prophets and Jesus. It reflects a change of heart and doesn't require a change in denomination.

"God Desires Everyone to Be Saved"

If the *Bible* teaches us that God "desires everyone to be saved" (1Tim 2:4), how can we doubt that God will accomplish this? Universalism sees God as the loving parent and presence that cares for *all*. Good parents love and discipline their children, but they do not reject or abandon them. Jesus taught that God is more loving than we imagine or that we can imagine (Matt 7:11). The effectiveness of God's discipline is best illustrated in the *Bible* by three famous murderers whom God forgave and later called into service to others: Moses, King David, and St. Paul. Moses was guilty of a "crime of passion" against an Egyptian (Ex 2:12). King David committed adultery with Bathsheba and then engineered the premeditated murder of her husband—one of his own soldiers (II Sam 11:14-26). St. Paul instigated a "hate crime" against St. Stephen, making him the first Christian martyr (Acts 7:58). Two vital lessons are being taught by these stories: God knows how rehabilitate people when humans fail, and God always forgives, even when humans won't.

In the Universalist understanding of theology, Hell is for rehabilitation and does not last forever. The famous 19th Century theologian Hosea Ballou taught that, "God saves men in order to purify them; that's what Salvation is designed for. God does not require men to be pure in order that he may save them." He went on to give this example: "Your child has fallen into the mire, and its body and garments are defiled. You cleanse it and array it in clean robes. The query is, 'Do you love your child because you have washed it? Or did you wash it because you loved it?'" God purifies us and saves us (Mal 3:2-3).

Anglican Bishop John Robinson notes that, "Christ in Origen's old words, remains on the Cross so long as one sinner remains in hell. This is not speculation: it is a statement grounded in the very necessity of God's nature." God is with us always, whether here or hereafter. As the psalmist notes, "If I ascend to heaven, you are there; if I make my bed in Sheol, you are there" (Ps 139:8). Jesus taught that we must be judged but that we can choose to go toward the light in life as in death. "God is light, and in him there is no darkness at all" (1 Jn 1:5).

Relationship to World Religions

Another significant contribution of the Universalist movement was a change toward the prevailing view of other world religions, i.e., if *all* are saved, other paths to God must have some validity!

Have you ever tuned into a Fundamentalist Christian television program and heard the twisted logic that Hitler is in Heaven because he was a Christian (he was Roman Catholic) but Gandhi is in Hell because he was a Hindu (actually he claimed to be a Hindu, Christian, Muslim and Jew all in one)? This is contrary to our innate sense of God's justice and the *New Testament*'s overwhelming mandate for us to *do* good. In the Synoptic Gospels of Matthew, Mark, and Luke,

Jesus teaches that Judgment for both Christians and non-Christians will be based on works (Matt 7:21).

"All Flesh Shall See the Salvation of God"

The chain of love never ends, and *all* are called to be part of it—Christian and non-Christian. With Jesus as Judge, no one is ever abandoned. Jesus tells us that the Kingdom of God is not only for the pure (Matt 5:8) but also for the impure (Matt 15:2; Lk 18:10-14), the pagan (Matt 15:21-28), and the heretic (Lk 10:25-37; Jn 4:16-30). Jesus' message to us is that we are *all* the sons and daughters of God (Matt 23:9; Jn 10:34-36). When we realize this, we can live in the Kingdom of God right now (Lk 17:20-21).

There are many ways to interpret the *Bible*, but Christians can be confident that the theology of Universal Restoration pervades this perennial best-seller! Rather than present a dry theological argument to advance the merits of Universalism, I want to highlight the simple joy of the Universalist message by using the words of the Biblical writers themselves. Within the following pages, you will discover the *Golden Thread* of Universalism in the *Bible*. Know that God's love for creation is unconditional, and after a **"time of trial"** (Matt 6:13) for some, there will be eventual salvation for *all* (I Tim 4:10). In time, "All flesh shall see the salvation of God" (Lk 3:6).

2

God's Promise of Universal Salvation in the Hebrew Scriptures

Modern Christians often find the *Hebrew Scriptures (Old Testament)* incompatible with the message of Jesus because of its portrayal of rudimentary people and a harsh God. However, the *Old Testament* becomes more palatable when we think of the *Bible* as relating a continually developing message. The early stories originated from primitive people whose concept of God was imperfectly developed. Moses provided some remedial rules to raise the basic standard of behavior. The Ten Commandments—simple enough for most elementary school children to understand today—prepared the people for hearing the high moral and spiritual messages of the latter prophets like Isaiah and, ultimately, Jesus. Jesus' ministry was to fulfill the Law (Matt 5:17). Grown beyond the childlike wards of Moses who were taught to "*be* good," the people listening to Jesus were commanded to "*do* good." Jesus elevated our understanding of God to a more mature level—an adult level. In other words, God remained unchanged throughout our journey together in the *Old Testament*, but our ability to perceive God gradually changed.

Over the millennia that the *Old Testament* stories were retold and finally written down, our early crude efforts to understand our relationship to God developed. By the time of the latter prophets like Isaiah, the strands that would become woven into the *Golden Thread* are more frequent, and the stern God of earlier times became the loving parent whose goodness extends to *all*. Isaiah foretells that *all* people will worship God (Is 40: 3-5; 45:22-24) and that God will save *all* the people (Is 52:10). He foresees a time when wars will be no more and when *all* people will come to feast at the table of God (Is 2:2, 4; 25:6-8). Writing in the 5th Century BCE, the prophet Malachi says that God realizes that people in other lands worship God although they call God by other names. In Malachi,

God tells our ancestors that God's "name is great among the nations" and that offerings are made to God throughout the world (Mal 1:11).

The *Bible* assures us that God is our own parent and the parent of the whole world. God is compassionate and merciful (Ps 145:8-9), and God's love endures forever (Ps 107:1; Lam 3:22). This is God's promise to *all*.

God's creation is good.
God saw everything that He had made, and indeed it was very good (Gen 1:31).

God is the parent of all.
Have we not all one Father? Has not one God created us (Mal 2:10)?

God's family is universal.
All the ends of the Earth shall remember and turn to the LORD; and all the families of the nations shall worship before him (Ps 22:27).

God is our guide.
Our steps are made firm by the Lord, when he delights in our way; though we stumble, we shall not fall headlong, for the Lord holds us up by the hand (Ps 37:23-24).

God is the one who saves us.
For God alone my soul waits in silence; from him comes my salvation (Ps 62:1).

ALL people will come to God.
All the nations you have made shall come and bow down before you, O Lord, and shall glorify your name (Ps 86:9).

God's goodness is unchanging.
Righteousness and justice are the foundation for your throne; steadfast love and faithfulness go before you (Ps 89:14).

God is the source of all.
O you who answer prayer! To you all flesh shall come (Ps 65:2).

God is great among the nations.
For from the rising of the sun to its setting my name is great among the nations, and in every place incense is offered to my name, and a pure offering; for my name is great among the nations, says the Lord of hosts (Mal 1:11).

God's love is everlasting.
O give thanks to the LORD, for He is good; for his steadfast love endures forever (Ps 107:1).

God is everywhere and with us always.
If I ascend to Heaven, you are there; if I make my bed in Sheol, you are there (Ps 139:8).

God is the Lord of all.
For I know their works and their thoughts, and I am coming to gather all nations and tongues; and they shall come and shall see my glory...All flesh shall come to worship before me, says the Lord (Is 66:18, 23).

God is merciful to all.
The Lord is gracious and merciful, slow to anger and abounding in steadfast love. The Lord is good to all, and his compassion is over all that he has made...The Lord upholds all who are falling, and raises up all who are bowed down (Ps 145:8-9, 14).

God is our salvation.
Surely God is my salvation; I will trust, and not be afraid, for the Lord God is my strength and my might; he has become my salvation (Is 12:2).

God's love removes barriers between peoples.
The Lord All-Powerful will prepare a feast on this mountain for all people. It will be a feast with all the best food and wine, the finest meat and wine. On this mountain God will destroy the veil that covers all nations, the veil that stretches over all peoples; he will destroy death forever. The Lord God will wipe away every tear from every face. He will take away the shame of his people from the earth. The Lord has spoken (Is 25:6-8, NCV).

God's love never ends.
The steadfast love of the Lord never ceases, his mercies never come to an end (Lam 3:22).

God will never abandon us.
Can a woman forget her nursing child, or show no compassion for the child of her womb? Even these may forget, yet I will not forget you (Is 49:15).

God's kingdom will come.
In days to come the mountain of the LORD'S house shall be established as the highest of the mountains, and shall be raised above the hills; and all the nations shall stream to it. He shall judge between the nations, and shall arbitrate for many peoples; they shall beat their swords into plowshares, and their spears into pruning hooks; nation shall not lift up sword against nation, neither shall they learn war anymore (Is 2:2 & 4).

God's peace will prevail.
They will not hurt or destroy on all my holy mountain; for the earth will be full of the knowledge of the LORD as the waters cover the sea (Is 11:9).

The day of the Lord will come.
A voice calls out: "In the wilderness prepare the way of the LORD, make straight in the desert a highway for our God. Every valley shall be lifted up, and every mountain and hill shall be made low; the uneven ground shall become level, and the rough places a plain. Then the glory of the LORD shall be revealed, and all people shall see it together, for the mouth of the LORD has spoken" (Is 40:3-5).

All *will know and serve God.*
Turn to me and be saved, all the ends of the Earth! For I am God, and there is no other. By myself I have sworn, from my mouth has gone forth in righteousness a word that shall not return: "To me every knee shall bow, every tongue shall swear." Only in the LORD, it shall be said of me, are righteousness and strength; all who were incensed against him shall come to him and be ashamed (Is 45:22-24).

God will save all.
The LORD has bared his holy arm before the eyes of all the nations; and all the ends of the earth shall see the salvation of our God (Is 52:10).

3

God's Promise of Forgiveness in the Hebrew Scriptures

Without the fear of Eternal damnation, what would prevent people from sinning with wild abandon? One of the arguments used against Universal Salvation in both ancient and modern times has been that if everyone goes to Heaven—as the Universalists claim—there would be no motivation to be good! Modern scientific research into human development, however, proves the opposite to be true. Love is a more powerful motivator than fear, and knowing that God is our ultimate parent inspires us to embrace the good and reject the bad.

Over a century ago, the minister and writer Edward Everett Hale wrote, "A child who is early taught that he is God's child, that he may live and move and have his being in God, and he has therefore, infinite strength at hand for conquering any difficulty, will take life more easily, and will probably make more of it, than one who is told that he is born the child of wrath and wholly incapable of good." This statement about the positive effects of knowing we are God's children is quoted in many books on the psychology of religion.

God is the parent of *all*, and God is the perfect parent. Just as the parent is more mature than the child, God is infinitely wiser than we are. Like a human parent, God counts on us, and our good works please God. When we fail to love our neighbor as ourselves, we let God down in the same way we let our loved ones down.

God disciplines but does not destroy (Ps 89:30-33; Ps 99:8; Ps 103:8-9), and the discipline of God makes us pure (Mal 3:2-3). God is forgiving, and God's anger is momentary (Is 12:1, 43:25, 54:8; Mic 7:18-19). God is our Redeemer (Hos 14:4), and God will never punish us beyond our endurance (Is 57:16; Lam 3:31-33). The pages of the *Bible* are God's developmental revelation to us, the children of God. As humanity has developed, so has our own understanding of God. The task of good religion is to make us aware that we are God's children.

When we realize that God is always with us, we can live our lives in conscious relationship with God.

Long before we were aware of it, God had compassion for us. The pages of the *Hebrew Scriptures* document our growing awareness of God's forgiveness. Only with the culmination of Law in the teachings of Jesus are people challenged to achieve a higher standard—to be as forgiving as God (Matt 6:12; Matt 5:45). Indeed, it becomes a requirement (Matt 6:14).

God is forgiving.
For his anger is but for a moment; his favor is for a lifetime (Ps 30:5).

God disciplines, but God's love is forever.
If his children forsake my law and do not walk according to my ordinances, if they violate my statutes and do not keep my commandments, then I will punish their transgression with the rod and their iniquity with scourges; but I will not remove from him my steadfast love, or be false to my faithfulness (Ps 89:30-33).

God is fair.
O LORD our God, you answer them; you were a forgiving God to them, but an avenger to their wrongdoings (Ps 99:8).

God is merciful.
The LORD is merciful and gracious, slow to anger and abounding in steadfast love. He will not always accuse, nor will he keep his anger forever (Ps 103:8-9).

God is a forgiving parent.
You will say in that day: I will give thanks to you, O LORD, for though you were angry with me, you turned your anger away, and you comforted me (Is 12:1).

God will cleanse us and make us obedient.
Then I will sprinkle clean water on you, and you will be clean. I will cleanse you from all your uncleanness and your idols. Also, I will teach you to respect me completely, and I will put a new way of thinking inside you. I will take out the stubborn hearts of stone from your bodies, and I will give you obedient hearts of flesh. I will put my Spirit inside you and help you live by my rules and carefully obey my laws (Ezek 36:25-27, NCV).

God purifies us and forgives us.
I, I am He who blots out your transgressions for my own sake, and I will not remember your sins (Is 43:25).

God is our Redeemer.
In an overflowing wrath for a moment I hid my face from you, but with everlasting love I will have compassion on you, says the LORD, your Redeemer (Is 54:8).

God will not test us beyond our strength.
For I will not continually accuse nor will I always be angry; for then the spirits would grow faint before me, even the souls that I have made (Is 57:16).

God is just and knows our heart.
For the LORD will not reject forever. Although He causes grief, he will have compassion according to the abundance of his steadfast love; for he does not willingly afflict or grieve anyone (Lam 3:31-33).

God is the one who saves us. God forgives though we have strayed.
Shall I ransom them from the power of Sheol? Shall I redeem them from death? O Death, where are your plagues? O Sheol, where is your destruction? Compassion is hidden from my eyes (Hos 13:14). I will heal their disloyalty; I will love them freely, for my anger has turned from them (Hos 14:4).

God is compassionate.
Who is a God like you, pardoning iniquity and passing over the transgression of the remnant of your possession? He does not retain his anger forever, because he delights in showing clemency. He will again have compassion upon us; he will tread our iniquities under foot. You will cast out all of our sins into the depth of the sea (Mic 7:18-19).

God promises us a new and better covenant and offers forgiveness to all.
"Look, the time is coming," says the Lord, "when I will make a new agreement with the people of Israel and the people of Judah. It will not be like the agreement I made with their ancestors when I took them by the hand to bring them out of Egypt. I was a husband to them, but they broke that agreement," says the Lord. "This is the agreement I will make with the people of Israel at that time," says the Lord: "I will put my teachings in their minds and write them on their hearts. I will be their God, and they will be my people. People will no longer have to teach their neighbors and relatives to know the Lord, because all people will know me, from the least to the most important," says the Lord. "I will forgive them for the wicked things they did, and I will not remember their sins anymore" (Jer 31:31-34, NCV).

God's discipline is for purification.
But who can endure the day of his coming, and who will stand when he appears? For he is like a refiner's fire and like a fuller's soap; he will sit as a refiner and purifier of silver, and he will purify the descendants of Levi and

refine them like gold and silver until they present offerings to the LORD in righteousness (Mal 3:2-3).

4

Judgment According to the New Testament

God's expectations for earliest humanity were minimal. Remember the account of Adam and Eve? God asks nothing more of his new creatures than that they "be fruitful" and avoid eating from a certain tree. After many years, God sent Moses with the Ten Commandments to raise a still-childlike people to a higher moral level. Time to internalize the Commandments given by Moses was needed before the people would become mature enough to hear Jesus, who talked of a more challenging Way. In the language of human development, Moses *had* to happen before Jesus *could* happen. If Jesus had appeared to the people of the Exodus saying, "Judge not", they would not have been able to comprehend him!

When we become adults, we do not throw out the basic rules of childhood; we build on them. The Laws of Moses were not obsolete but incomplete, and Jesus' mission was to fulfill the Law (Matt 5:17). The laws that Jesus (and later St. Paul) sought to abolish were Jewish Ritual Laws—those meticulous ceremonies observed to insure "purity." To Jesus, some of the most "pious" in Jewish society had lost their perspective in the minutia of these rituals; Jesus taught that God wanted more from us than mechanical observance of ritual. Jesus was not kosher in his eating and drinking habits. He ate with people who were unclean (Matt 11:19) and violated many aspects of Jewish Ritual Law (Matt 15:1-20; 23:23-25).

Jesus' teachings beckon us toward a new dimension in our relationship to God that is best exemplified by his teachings in the Sermon on the Mount (Matt 5:1-7:29). He encouraged a religion based on genuine love for ourselves and others. By following the teachings of Jesus, we are lead into the Kingdom of God, not only in the Hereafter but in the here-and-now. Jesus set a much tougher standard than Moses: Don't just *be* good, *do* good. Jesus showed us the Way through his teachings of Truth and Life (Jn 14:6).

In Jesus' great teaching called "The Judgment of the Nations" (Matt 25:31-46), we are shown the path to salvation traveled by both Christians and non-Christians. Other major religions also teach the "Golden Rule" and the importance of good works. "The Judgment of the Nations" (Matt 25:31-46) highlights the universality of Jesus' message in the words, **"All the Nations,"** making it clear that Salvation is intended for both Christians and non-Christians who do good. St. Peter says, "I truly understand that God shows no partiality, but in every nation anyone who fears Him and does what is right is acceptable to Him" (Acts 10:34-35). Do other religions have paths to Salvation? Those who believe in a loving God say, "Yes." Why would Jesus remind us that God wants us to **"Love your neighbor as yourself"** (Matt 22:39) and then not love *all* of us? Why would God leave so much of the world in darkness? **"God is Light, and in Him there is no darkness"** (I Jn 1:5) and "God is Love" (I Jn 4:8).

Judgment is based on deeds done "to the least of these" rather to adherence to a dogmatic formula of belief. "Belief in Jesus" brings Salvation only if it leads to a change in heart and behavior (Matt 7:21). One of the most important things Jesus taught about Judgment is that it is *not our job* to judge others (Matt 7:1-2). It's God's job—not your relative's, your neighbor's, your preacher's or your bishop's! The *Bible* cautions us that God has an entirely different standard for judging us than we have for judging each other (Jn 5:22, 8:15). So beware of people who try to "keep score" of your good deeds; only God can do that!

Jesus teaches that good deeds reveal one's spirit more than empty words.
Not everyone who says to me, 'Lord, Lord' will enter the kingdom of heaven, but only the one who does the will of my Father in heaven (Matt 7:21).

Jesus teaches that our words are also judged.
The good person brings good things out of a good treasure, and the evil person brings evil things out of an evil treasure. I tell you, on the day of judgment you will have to give an account for every careless word you utter; for by your words you will be justified, and by your words you will be condemned (Matt 12:35-37).

Jesus teaches that good deeds will be rewarded at judgment.
For the Son of Man is to come with his angels in the glory of his Father, and then he will repay everyone for what has been done (Matt 16:27).

Jesus tells his disciples that all secrets will become known.
Nothing is covered up that will not be uncovered, and nothing secret that will not become known. Therefore whatever you have said in the dark will be heard in the light, and what you have whispered behind closed doors will be proclaimed from the housetops (Lk 12:2-3).

In Jesus' parable of the Rich Man and Lazarus, he illustrates the concepts of immediate judgment and life after death based on good works. Note that the rich man's request to warn his brothers indicates that rehabilitation has already begun, as he is showing concern for others.
There was a rich man who always dressed in the finest clothes and lived in luxury every day. And a very poor man named Lazarus, whose body was covered with sores, was laid at the rich man's gate. He wanted to eat only the small pieces of food that fell from the rich man's table. And the dogs would come and lick his sores. Later, Lazarus died, and the angels carried him to the arms of Abraham. The rich man died, too, and was buried. In the place of the dead, he was in much pain. The rich man saw Abraham far away with Lazarus at his side. He called, "Father Abraham, have mercy on me! Send Lazarus to dip his finger in water and cool my tongue, because I am suffering in this fire!" But Abraham said, "Child, remember when you were alive you had the good things in life, but bad things happened to Lazarus. Now he is comforted here, and you are suffering. Besides, there is a big pit between you and us, so no one can cross over to you, and no one can leave there and come here." The rich

man said, "Father, then please send Lazarus to my father's house. I have five brothers, and Lazarus could warn them so that they will not come to this place of pain." But Abraham said, "They have the law of Moses and the writings of the prophets; let them learn from them." The rich man said, "No, father Abraham! If someone goes to them from the dead, they would believe and change their hearts and lives." But Abraham said to him, "If they will not listen to Moses and the prophets, they will not listen to someone who comes back from the dead" (Lk 16:19-31, NCV).

In Jesus' strongest statement regarding salvation by works, note that Jesus himself is the Judge and that he uses the same standard of good works to judge both Christians and non-Christians.

The Son of Man will come again in his great glory, with all his angels. He will be King and sit on his great throne. All the nations of the world will be gathered before him, and he will separate them into two groups as a shepherd separates the sheep from the goats. The Son of Man will put the sheep on his right and the goats on his left. Then the King will say to the people on his right, "Come, my Father has given you his blessing. Receive the kingdom God has prepared for you since the world was made. I was hungry, and you gave me food. I was thirsty, and you gave me something to drink. I was alone and away from home, and you invited me into your house. I was without clothes, and you gave me something to wear. I was sick, and you cared for me. I was in prison, and you visited me." Then the good people will answer, "Lord, when did we see you hungry and give you food, or thirsty and give you something to drink? When did we see you alone and away from home and invite you into our house? When did we see you without clothes and give you something to wear? When did we see you sick or in prison and care for you?" Then the King will answer, "I tell you the truth, anything you did for even the least of my people here, you also did for me." Then the King will say to those on his left, "Go away from me. You will be punished. Go into the fire that burns forever that was prepared for the devil and his angels. I was hungry, and you gave me nothing to eat. I was thirsty, and you gave me nothing to drink. I was alone and away from home, and you did not invite me into your house. I was without clothes, and you gave me nothing to wear. I was sick and in prison, and you did not care for me." Then those people will answer, "Lord, when did we see you hungry or thirsty or alone and away from home or without clothes or sick or in prison? When did we see these things and not

help you?" Then the King will answer, "I tell you the truth, anything you refused to do for even the least of my people here, you refused to do for me." These people will go off to be punished forever, but the good people will go to live forever" (Matt 25:31-46, NCV).

After Jesus' death and resurrection, his followers continued to preach his message of salvation by good works and salvation for all peoples.

Peter
I truly understand that God shows no partiality, but in every nation anyone who fears him and does what is right is acceptable to him (Acts 10:34-35).

The Lord knows how to rescue the godly from trial, and to keep the unrighteous under punishment until the day of judgment (II Peter 2:9).

Paul
For he will repay according to each one's deeds (Rom 2:6).

For God shows no partiality (Rom 2:11).

Why do you pass judgment on your brother or sister? Or you, why do you despise your brother or sister? For we will all stand before the judgment seat of God. For it is written, "As I live, says the Lord, every knee shall bow to me, and every tongue shall give praise to God." So then, each of us will be accountable to God (Rom 14:10-12).

Therefore do not pronounce judgment before the time, before the Lord comes, who will bring to light the things now hidden in darkness and will disclose the purposes of the heart. Then each one will receive commendation from God (I Cor 4:5).

For all of us must appear before the judgment seat of Christ, so that each may receive recompense for what has been done in the body, whether good or evil (II Cor 5:10).

Do not be deceived; God is not mocked, for you reap whatever you sow (Gal 6:7).

For the wrongdoer will be paid back for whatever wrong has been done, and there is no partiality (Col 3:25).

James (The Brother of Jesus)
So faith by itself, if it has no works, is dead. But someone will say, "You have faith and I have works." Show me your faith apart from your works, and I by

my works will show you my faith. You believe that God is one; you do well. Even the demons believe—and shudder (Jas 2:17-19).

John (written in exile on the Island of Patmos)
And I saw the dead, great and small, standing before the throne, and books were opened. Also another book was opened, the book of life. And the dead were judged according to their works, as recorded in the books (Rev 20:12).

5

Hell Is for Rehabilitation

How is Universal Salvation possible when descriptions in the *Bible* of Judgment and Hell are so explicit? Universal Salvation is compatible with Judgment and Hell because of one of the least-known concepts in the Biblical text—Hell is not permanent. Verses from both the *Old Testament* and *New Testament* make a convincing case that God uses Hell for our rehabilitation and that after a "**time of trial**" (Matt 6:13), *all* will be saved (I Tim 4:10).

If Hell is not really "Eternal", what does Jesus mean when he says in the "Judgment of the Nations" that the "goats" will be **"punished forever"** (Matt 25:46)? Universalist scholar Prof. Thomas Talbott notes that the Greek word for *forever* is better understood as "that which pertains to an age." For example, when Jonah was swallowed by the great fish, he "went down to the land whose bars closed on me *forever*" (Jonah 2:6, *emphasis added*). However, this story ends when Jonah is released by God from his bondage after just three days. In three other instances—his parable of the unforgiving servant (Matt 18:34-35) and his descriptions of a prisoner's fate (Matt 5:25-26, Lk 12:57-59)—Jesus indicates that punishment is not eternal but lasts only until you pay your **"entire debt"** (Matt 18:34). It also is worth noting that Jesus often exaggerates to make his point, e.g., **"If your right eye causes you to sin, tear it out...if your right hand causes you to sin, cut it off..."** (Matt 5:29-30).

Over the past few decades, increasing numbers of modern people have described a personal, direct knowledge of Hell as the result of their "near-death experience" (people revived following a period of clinical death). Interestingly, those who found themselves in Hell initially often reversed their experience from negative to positive when they called out to God or Jesus. These encounters seem to indicate that God still rescues people.

The *Bible* is clear that Jesus went to Hell to rescue people who had not obeyed God prior to their death (I Pet 3:18-20; 4:6). These verses from 1st Peter have been important for Universalist theology since ancient times, as they clearly indicate that Eternal Hell is not God's wish.

If you were God, would you choose to damn people to Eternal Hell when you had the power to rehabilitate them? If we define God as all good, we must assume that even the most incorrigible of human beings will eventually acknowledge the truth and come to God. So we'd better make peace with our neighbors now, since we will *all* be meeting again in the Hereafter!

In Jesus' parable of the Wicked Servant, Jesus clarifies his teaching in the Lord's Prayer that we must forgive others to merit God's forgiveness of us. The servant's master is compassionate toward him and forgives a large debt, but the wicked servant is unforgiving toward a fellow servant whose debt to him is small. The wicked slave is not punished forever, but only until he pays his debt. The parable ends by saying that God will do the same to us if we are not forgiving.

Then his lord summoned him and said to him, "You wicked slave! I forgave you all that debt because you pleaded with me. Should you not have had mercy on your fellow slave, as I had mercy on you?" And in anger his lord handed him over to be tortured until he would pay his entire debt. So my heavenly Father will also do to every one of you, if you do not forgive your brother or sister from your heart (Matt 18:32-35).

Jesus tells his disciples that people are capable of distinguishing right from wrong and should not require the threat of authority to do the right thing. Inevitably, God's punishment of wrongdoers will last until they understand this.

And why do you not judge for yourselves what is right? Thus, when you go with your accuser before a magistrate, on the way make an effort to settle the case, or you may be dragged before the judge, and the judge hand you over to the officer, and the officer throw you in prison. I tell you, you will never get out until you have paid the very last penny. (Luke 12:57-59, also Matt 5:25-26)

Those who have been taught good religion are more responsible for their actions.

The slave who knew what his master wanted, but did not prepare himself or do what was wanted, will receive a severe beating. But the one who did not know and did what deserved a beating will receive a light beating (Luke 12:47-48).

After his death, Jesus went to preach to those in Hell. God loves us—even in Hell—and will save us all *eventually.*

When it says, "He ascended," what does it mean but that he also descended into the lower parts of the earth? He who descended is the same one who ascended far above all the Heavens so that he might fill all things (Eph 4:9-10).

For Christ also suffered for sins once for all, the righteous for the unrighteous, in order to bring you to God. He was put to death in the flesh, but made alive in the spirit, in which also he went and made a proclamation to the spirits in prison, who in former times did not obey (I Pet 3:18-20). For this is the reason the gospel was proclaimed even to the dead, so that, though they had been judged in the flesh as everyone is judged, they might live in the spirit as God does (I Pet 4:6).

Paul implies that some people will require some "shaping up" before they are saved!
When we are judged by the Lord, we are disciplined (I Cor 11:32).

God knows our assets and limitations.
God is faithful, and he will not let you be tested beyond your strength, but with the testing he will also provide the way out so that you may be able to endure it (I Cor 10:13).

God does not want us to perish.
If what has been built on the foundation survives, the builder will receive a reward. If the work is burned up, the builder will suffer loss; the builder will be saved, but only as through fire (I Cor 3:14-15).

Just as the Old Testament *prophet Malachi states that God purifies us with fire to save us (Mal 3:2-3), so does the* New Testament *author of Hebrews.*
Our God is a consuming fire (Heb 12:29).

John the Baptist emphasizes that fire is for purification.
He *(Jesus)* will baptize you with the Holy Spirit and fire (Lk 3:16).

This idea is reiterated in Jesus' teaching.
I came to bring fire to the earth, and how I wish it were already kindled! (Lk 12:49). **For everyone will be salted with fire** (Mk 9:49).

*Hell is a place of discipline for some, but after a **"time of trial,"** all will be saved.*
And you have forgotten the exhortation that addresses you as children—"My child, do not regard lightly the discipline of the Lord, or lose heart when you are punished by him; for the Lord disciplines those who he loves and chastises every child whom he accepts" (Heb 12:5-6). Moreover, we had human parents and respected them. Should we not be even more willing to be subject to the Father of spirits and live? For they disciplined us for a short time as seemed best to them, but he disciplines us for our good, in order that we may share his holiness (Heb 12:9-10).

6

Universal Salvation According to the New Testament

Almost all Christians learn to memorize "The Lord's Prayer," probably the most familiar part of the rich body of Jesus' teachings known as the "Sermon on the Mount." Too often we catch ourselves mechanically reciting its opening words, **"Our Father"** (Matt 6:9), without appreciating their amazing assertion. In Jesus' own words, he tells us that—of all the lofty names we might consider magnificent enough to address the Almighty—we should approach God like a child does her parent. Jesus had a genuine relationship to God and showed us the Way to foster a similar kind of personal connection to Our Father. Jesus calls God "Abba," a term so affectionate that it is thought to mean something like "Daddy." After Jesus' death, he appeared to Mary Magdalene using poignant words revealing his knowledge that His Father and Our Father are the same: **"I am ascending to my Father and your Father..."** (Jn 20:17). For Jesus, God was not a distant tyrant but an ever-present, loving reality who raised our species up from its childlike beginnings and who continues to guide us.

Jesus taught that we are the children of God (Jn 10:33-36), that God already loves us (I Jn 4:8), and that God knows what we need before we ask (Matt 6:8). Jesus fills his ministry with requirements that sound simple initially but are ultimately very challenging: treat others the way we want to be treated, forgive, and do not judge others. Over and over, Jesus attempted to describe what the Kingdom of God is like to his disciples and the crowds; curiously, he claimed that the Kingdom of God is *within us* (Lk17:20-21)! Because of Jesus' reverent submission to God, God raised him and made him Lord and Messiah (Heb 5:7-10; Acts 2: 32-36; Eph 1:20).

The case for Universalism in the *Bible* is best illustrated by Jesus in his Parables of the Lost Sheep, the Lost Coin, and the Prodigal Son (Matt 18:10-14; Lk 15:1-32). In the Parable of the Lost Sheep, the ninety-nine sheep safely in the fold represent the majority of humanity that has already been judged worthy. The wayward sheep does not make any effort to find its own way back to the others. It is the shepherd (God) who takes an active role in searching for the one that has wandered off, just as God continuously seeks after humans who stray. Jesus says, **"It is not the will of your Father in heaven that one of these little ones should be lost"** (Matt 18:14).

The Parable of the Lost Coin also demonstrates God's will that *all* be saved. Here the woman in the story (God) knows that the nine remaining coins are already safe. She makes a valiant effort to search until she finds the missing one. We are all in God's inventory of Divine possessions, and God's search will go on until each of us is "found." There is no time limit placed on how much time it takes. It may occur here or in the Hereafter, but we are assured that it will happen "in the fullness of time" (Eph 1:10). We have God's love here and in the Hereafter (Acts 17:28; Rom 11:36; Eph 4:6). The Hereafter is the state in which we remain in the light and love of God.

In the story of the Prodigal Son, the son has suffered as the result of his own actions. The father (God) welcomes his son back into the family with open arms.

Hell as depicted in literature and art reflects the hardness of the human heart and not the compassion of a loving God who is the parent of *all*. Because we judge harshly, we can envision a place of endless punishment, but Universalism recognizes a Hell grounded in Scripture where *rehabilitation* is the priority.

Some may wonder: If *all* are to be saved either immediately or eventually, what do Universalists get out of being religious in their everyday lives? Universalists treasure the knowledge that "the Lord is my shepherd, I shall not want" (Ps 23:1). We rejoice in knowing that we are in God's fold.

Jesus tells us that God is good to *all*, loves *all*, and will redeem *all* (Matt 5:45, 18:12-14). When one thinks of the loving God that Jesus talked about, could it be any other way? In the words of the famous 19th Century Universalist theologian Hosea Ballou, "What the Mediator (Jesus) did for sinners was the consequence and not the cause of God's love to us." Pearly Silloway, a 20th Century Universalist theologian notes that, "We may safely aver that all rational creatures will ultimately arrive at the condition of harmony with divine love, both because the Father so desires it, and because each individual's own volition will direct his steps homeward."

If God desires everyone to be saved (I Tim 2:3-6), does anyone doubt that this will happen? Our lives on Earth are temporary, but our relationship with God is forever. In the end, we will *all* be united with God, and God will be "all in all" (I

Cor 15:28). When one sees God as the ultimate parent, Universal Restoration is the only outcome possible.

The Prophet Daniel says that the Son of Man will rule over "all peoples."
In my vision at night I saw in front of me someone who looked like a human being (Son of Man) coming on the clouds in the sky. He came near God who has been alive forever, and he was led to God. He was given authority, glory, and the strength of a king. People of every tribe, nation, and language will serve him. His rule will last forever, and his kingdom will never be destroyed (Dan 7:13-14, NCV).

At the birth of Jesus, the angel of the Lord tells the shepherds that Jesus will be the Messiah for "all the people."
But the angel said to them, "Do not be afraid; for see—I am bringing you good news of great joy for all the people" (Lk 2:10).

When Jesus was presented at the Temple at age eight days, Simeon—a devout Jew who had been told by the Holy Spirit that he would not die before he saw the Messiah—recognizes Jesus as the one promised.
Master, now you are dismissing your servant in peace, according to your word; for my eyes have seen your salvation, which you have prepared in the presence of all peoples, a light for revelation to the Gentiles and for glory to your people Israel (Lk 2:29-32).

John the Baptist quotes the prophet Isaiah (Is 40:5).
All flesh shall see the salvation of God (Lk 3:6).

Jesus tells us that God is good to all.
For he makes his sun rise on the evil and on the good, and sends rain on the righteous and on the unrighteous (Matt 5:45).

One of Jesus' most poignant parables about Universal Salvation is the Parable of the Lost Sheep. In Matthew, God (the Good Shepherd) seeks and saves the lost sheep; the sheep does not return to the flock of its own accord. The parable ends, **"…it is not the will of your Father in Heaven that one of these little ones should be lost."**
What do you think? If a shepherd has a hundred sheep, and one of them has gone astray, does he not leave the ninety-nine on the mountains and go in search of the one that went astray? And if he finds it, truly I tell you, he rejoices over it more than over the ninety-nine that never went astray. So it is not the will of your Father in heaven that one of these little ones should be lost (Matt 18:12-14).

This meaning of the Parable of the Lost Sheep is reiterated in the Parable of the Lost Coin. In it, the woman (God) searches until the coin is recovered.

Suppose a woman has ten silver coins, but loses one. She will light a lamp, sweep the house, and look carefully for the coin until she finds it. And when she finds it, she will call her friends and neighbors and say, "Be happy with me because I have found the coin that I lost" (Lk 15:8-9, NCV).

God's standards—not ours—will determine our place in the Kingdom. God's love is that of our ultimate parent, and God loves those whom we humans may consider undeserving. In the Parable of the Laborers in the Vineyard, Jesus shows that God is merciful to all. When we think of Mother Theresa as a worker who arrived early in the day, it is easier for most of us to admit that we showed up a bit later!

The kingdom of heaven is like a person who owned some land. One morning, he went out very early to hire some people to work in his vineyard. The man agreed to pay the workers one coin for working that day. Then he sent them into the vineyard to work. About nine o'clock the man went to the marketplace and saw some other people standing there, doing nothing. So he said to them, "If you go and work in my vineyard, I will pay you what your work is worth."...So they went to work in the vineyard...The man went out again about twelve o'clock...three o'clock...five o'clock...The man said to them, "Then you can go and work in my vineyard." At the end of the day, the owner of the vineyard said to the boss of all the workers, "Call the workers and pay them. Start with the last people I hired and end with those I hired first." When the workers who were hired at five o'clock came to get their pay, each received one coin. When the workers who were hired first came to get their pay, they thought they would be paid more than the others. But each one of them also received one coin. When they got their coin, they complained to the man who owned the land. They said, "Those people were hired last and worked only one hour. But you paid them the same as you paid us who worked hard all day in the hot sun." But the man who owned the vineyard said to one of those workers, "Friend, I am being fair to you. You agreed to work for one coin. So take your pay and go. I want to give the man who was hired last the same pay that I gave you. I can do what I want with my own money. Are you jealous because I am good to those people?" (Matt 20:1-15, NCV)

God's grace is beyond our comprehension.
For mortals it is impossible, but not for God; for God all things are possible (Mk 10:27).

God is compassionate and merciful.
He is kind to the ungrateful and the wicked (Lk 6:35).

In the story of the Prodigal Son, the returning son does not ask to be a member of the family but for a job as his father's servant. It is the father (God) who takes him back into the family. The father is the character with the active role. People often have difficulty with this story because they wrongly identify with the good son and not with the father. Considering how much human parents love their children, the story puts some perspective on how much God, who is all good, loves each of us.

A man had two sons. The younger son said to his father, "Give me my share of the property." So the father divided the property between his two sons. Then the younger son gathered up all that was his and traveled far away to another country. There he wasted his money in foolish living. After he had spent everything, a time came when there was no food anywhere in the country, and the son was poor and hungry. So he got a job with one of the citizens there who sent the son into the fields to feed pigs. The son was so hungry that he wanted to eat the pods the pigs were eating, but no one gave him anything. When he realized what he was doing, he thought, "All of my father's servants have plenty of food. But I am here, almost dying with hunger. I will leave and return to my father and say to him, 'Father, I have sinned against God and have done wrong to you. I am no longer worthy to be called your son, but let me be like one of your servants.'" So the son left and went to his father. While the son was still a long way off, his father saw him and felt sorry for his son. So the father ran to him and hugged and kissed him. The son said, "Father, I have sinned against God and have done wrong to you. I am no longer worthy to be called your son." But the father said to his servants, "Hurry! Bring the best clothes and put them on him. Also put a ring on his finger and sandals on his feet. And get our fat calf and kill it so we can have a feast and celebrate. My son was dead, but now he is alive again! He was lost, but now he is found!" So they began to celebrate. The older son was in the field, and as he came closer to the house, he heard the sound of music and dancing. So he called to one of the servants and asked what all this meant. The servant said, "Your brother has

come back, and your father killed the fat calf because your brother came home safely." The older son was angry and would not go in to the feast. So his father went out and begged him to come in. But the older son said to his father, "I have served you like a slave for many years and have always obeyed your commands. But you never gave me even a young goat to have a feast with my friends. But your other son, who wasted all your money on prostitutes, comes home, and you kill the fat calf for him!" The father said to him, "Son, you are always with me, and all that I have is yours. We had to celebrate and be happy because your brother was dead, but now he is alive. He was lost, but now he is found" (Lk 15:11-32, NCV).

The mission of Jesus is to all.
For the Son of Man came to seek out and save the lost (Lk 19:10).

Jesus tells us his message of God's universal love and forgiveness is an easy one to understand and one in which we can take comfort.
Come to me, all you that are weary and are carrying heavy burdens, and I will give you rest. Take my yoke upon you, and learn from me; for I am gentle and humble in heart, and you will find rest for your souls. For my yoke is easy, and my burden is light (Matt 11:28-30).

From the Mystic Gospel of John:

John the Baptist recognizes Jesus as the Messiah.
Here is the Lamb of God who takes away the sin of the world (Jn 1:29).

Jesus proclaims that God has sent him on a mission of reconciliation.
God did not send the son into the world to condemn the world, but in order that the world might be saved through him (Jn 3:17).

The heretics (Samaritans) are among the first to realize Jesus' mission to all.
We know that this is truly the Savior of the world (Jn 4:42).

Jesus tells us that God does not judge us (Acts 17:31; I Tim 2:5).
The Father judges no one but has given all judgment to the Son (Jn 5:22).

But Jesus does not judge us either, at least in the way we think of judgment on Earth.
You judge by human standards; I judge no one (Jn 8:15).

Jesus' flock includes non-Christians.
I have other sheep that do no belong to this fold. I must bring them also, and they will listen to my voice. So there will be one flock, one shepherd (Jn 10:16).

We are all to know God's laws.
It is written in the prophets, "And they will all be taught by God" (Jn 6:45).

Jesus is the shepherd of us all.
After Jesus had spoken these words, he looked up to Heaven and said, **"Father, the hour has come; glorify your Son so that the Son may glorify you, since you have given him authority over all people, to give eternal life to all whom you have given him"** (Jn 17:1-2).

Jesus will unite us all with God.
And I, when I am lifted up from the earth, will draw all people to myself (Jn 12:32).

After his death, Jesus appeared to Mary Magdalene, and assures her that God is the parent of us all.
I am ascending to my Father and your Father, to my God and your God (Jn 20:17).

Universal Salvation Reiterated by Other *New Testament* Authors

Jesus leads us to God.
Therefore just as one man's trespass led to condemnation for all, so one man's act of righteousness leads to justification and life for all (Rom 5:18).

Jesus has ushered in the Kingdom of God.
For creation waits with eager longing for the revealing of the children of God; for the creation was subjected to futility, not of its own will but by the will of the one who subjected it, in hope that the creation itself will be set free from its bondage to decay and will obtain the freedom of the glory of the children of God (Rom 8:19-21).

God loves us and is with us always and Jesus, through his teachings, has shown us the Way.
Yes, I am sure that neither death, nor life, nor angels, nor ruling spirits, nothing now, nothing in the future, no powers, nothing above us, nothing below us, nor anything else in the whole world will ever be able to separate us from the love of God that is in Christ Jesus our Lord (Rom 8:38-39, NCV).

We are accountable to God, but God is merciful.
For God has imprisoned all in disobedience so that he may be merciful to all (Rom 11:32).

We all return to God.
For from him and through him and to him are all things (Rom 11:36).

Though we are mortal we will all be raised up to be with God in a "spiritual body" (I Cor 15:44).
For as all die in Adam, so all will be made alive in Christ (I Cor 15:22).

God raised Jesus and made him mediator (I Tim 2:5; Heb 8:6).
When all things are subjected to him then the Son himself will also be subjected to the one who put all things in subjection under him, so that God may be all in all (I Cor 15:28).

Our souls are all *in the image of God.*
All of us with unveiled faces, seeing the glory of the Lord as though reflected in a mirror, are being transformed into the same image from one degree of glory to another; for this comes from the Lord, the Spirit (II Cor 3:18).

We are the messengers of God's promise of Universalism.
In Christ God was reconciling the world to himself, not counting their trespasses against them, and entrusting the message of reconciliation to us (II Cor 5:19).

God is with us always.
One God and Father of all who is above all and through all and in all (Eph 4:6).

God wants everyone to be saved. If God desires this, can anyone doubt that it will happen?
This is right and is acceptable in the sight of God our Savior, who desires everyone to be saved and to come to the knowledge of the truth. For there is one God; there is also one mediator between God and humankind, Christ Jesus, himself human, who gave himself a ransom for all (I Tim 2:3-6).

Jesus is an advocate and mediator between humans and God for both Christians and non-Christians.
My little children, I am writing these things to you so that you may not sin. But if anyone does sin, we have an advocate with the Father, Jesus Christ, the righteous; and he is the atoning sacrifice for our sins, and not for ours only but also for the sins of the whole world (I Jn 2:1-2).

God is Savior of all. This is the great message of Universalism.
For to this end we toil and struggle, because we have our hope set on the living God, who is the Savior of all people, especially of those who believe (I Tim 4:10).

God teaches and God forgives.
The Holy Spirit also testifies to us, for after saying, "This is the covenant that I will make with them after those days, says the Lord: I will put my laws in their hearts, and I will write them on their minds," he also adds, "I will remember their sins and their lawless deeds no more" (Heb 10:15-17).

God is patient and wants all *to be saved.*
The Lord is not slow about his promise, as some think of slowness, but is patient with you not wanting any to perish, but all to come to repentance (II Pet 3:9).

God is Universal Goodness.
Every precious act of giving, with every perfect gift, is from above, coming down from the Father of lights, with whom there is no variation or shadow due to change (Jas 1:17).

Jesus message to us is that God is the Savior of all.
He has made known to us the mystery of his will, according to his good pleasure that he set forth in Christ, as a plan for the fullness of time, to gather up all things in him, things in heaven and things on earth (Eph 1:9-10).

Universal Salvation is God's gift to humanity.
For the grace of God has appeared, bringing salvation to all (Titus 2:11).

7

Mystical Religious Experiences and Christian Universalism

The very personal, direct experience of God—when the barriers between the human being and God's Universe dissolve—is termed a mystical religious experience. Both the *Hebrew Scriptures* and the *New Testament* tell of many who were immersed in the Spirit of God. Within their pages, we are allowed to share the visions of God through the eyes of the Prophet Isaiah (Is 1:1, 6:1-8) and to enter into the ecstatic mystical experience as told by St. Paul (II Cor 12:2). For Christians, Jesus is the one who most perfectly became One with God (Jn 10:30). In addition to those named in the *Bible*, "saints", "sages", and "mystics" blessed with this intimate knowledge of God have existed from the beginning of time, and we are fortunate to have the writings of many who were emboldened to act in their societies following their experiences. (Later in this chapter, some of the well-known Universalist mystics will be discussed.) But were you aware that religious mystics are still among us today? Over the past hundred years, researchers in the scientific study of religion have been able to determine that "mystical" experiences of God are not really so rare! (Data from this scientific inquiry will be explored later in this chapter.) When I have taught adult Sunday school classes or Psychology of Religion classes on the topic of mystical religious experience, inevitably those who can recall their own mystical experience of God understand me perfectly while those who have not had this kind of personal experience often remain skeptical! In this chapter, I hope to offer some personal and social science evidence which will help to expand the understanding of this phenomenon.

To me, the fact that everyone has not had a personal mystical experience is a source of sadness. The great dream of all mystics is that we could, in the words of William Blake, "cleanse the doors of perception" so that all might experience directly the loving presence of God in the here-and-now. In reality, "unknown" and "anonymous" mystics have been discovered among ordinary people in almost half the population. Two more facts regarding mystical experiences help to put this experience into perspective: The first is that mystical religious experiences usually occur only once or twice in the lifetimes of about half of those reporting them, and the second is that mystical religious experiences, although always profound, definitely vary in intensity from one person to another. Some years ago I was watching a television interview of Mother Theresa who related that she had only *one* mystical experience—a vision of Jesus telling her to go to India and serve the poor! When I teach, I often make the analogy that some of us received a *candle* of light while Jesus received a *beacon*!

Mystical religious experiences are categorized as either "spontaneous" (they "just happen!") or "sought-after." Meditation is the *only* safe way to induce this experience, but there is no guarantee that meditation will produce the desired outcome.

All true mystical experiences serve to reinforce what Jesus taught about God's love for us. Mystics through the ages have reminded us to stay the true course, reject dogma, and not let mechanical ritual substitute for good works and kindness. Like Jesus, Christian mystics have often been at odds with the church leaders when those leaders have put authority, church business, and theological interpretation above the compassion of God.

Jesus promised the continuous presence of the Holy Spirit (Jn 14:26), and St. Paul expressed his unquestioned belief that the direct experience of God is open to everyone (II Cor 3:18). Conservative Christian scholar Luke Timothy Johnson correctly notes that mystical religious experiences described in the *New Testament* are often ignored in modern studies of Christian origins. This direct contact between God and humanity in the *New Testament* is also discussed by moderate Christian scholar James D. G. Dunn, in his book *Jesus and the Spirit*.

Universalism Among Mystics

Universalist theology is rooted in religious mystical experience and can be found in mystics writing as early as the 2nd Century and continuing throughout the Dark Ages, the Reformation, and the Age of Enlightenment. Mystic and researcher Evelyn Underhill considers these prominent Universalist mystics to be among the greatest: Clement of Alexandria (160-220), Origen (183-253), Macarius of Egypt (295-386), Gregory of Nyssa (335-394), John Scotus Erigena (810-877), Jacob Boehme (1575-1624), and Jane Lead(e) (1625-1704). The Carmelite Priest and mystical researcher Bruno Borchert adds these Universalists: Gregory of Nazianze (329-390) and Hans Denck (1500-1527). In my view, no list of

Universalist mystics would be complete without George De Benneville (1703-1793).

Jane Lead, who founded a society of Universalists called the Philadelphians in 17th Century London, described her mystical experience in which the nature of post-mortem punishment was revealed to her. Recorded in her book, *The Enochian Walks with God*, she states that God's love triumphs, that punishment is for reforming, and that all are reconciled with God in the end. George De Benneville—physician, preacher, and mystic—wrote of his Universalist mystical religious experience and his in-depth near-death experience in his book entitled, *The Life and Trance of Dr. George De Benneville*. Like Jane Lead, these personal experiences convinced De Benneville that Hell is for purification and that, in the end, *all* will be united with God.

Throughout the history of Christianity, mystics not identified formally as Universalists have nevertheless advocated Universalist ideas. This is hardly surprising, as in the West the Catholic Church had condemned Origen's form of Universalism as heretical, and Universalism had to go underground until the Reformation. In contrast, the Eastern Church (Oriental Orthodox, a.k.a. Nestorian Church or Assyrian Church of the East) accepted Universalist theology. Greats such as Theodore of Mopsuestia placed Universalism solidly in the liturgy. Additionally, Universalism is recorded in the Eastern Church's 13th Century *Book of the Bee* (Chapter LX). Universalist thinking continues in less emphatic form in the liturgy of the Eastern Church today.

A good example of Universalism in the writings of "unofficial" Universalist mystics is the great 14th Century English mystic, Julian of Norwich. Though her Universalist mystical experiences of God were contrary to Catholic Church teachings of Hell and Purgatory, she wrote that both must be true in some sense, though she did not see it. This "dance" she did between church dogma and her mystical religious experiences was enough to keep her in the good graces of church officials. Nevertheless, her Universalism shines through. She writes:

> All shall be well, and all shall be well, and all manner of thing shall be well...And He is very Father and very Mother of Nature: and all natures that He hath made to flow out of Him to work His will shall be restored and brought again into Him by the salvation of man through the working of Grace...All this being so, it seemed to me that it was impossible that every kind of thing should be well, as our Lord revealed at this time...And to this I had no other answer as a revelation from our Lord except this: "What is impossible to you is not impossible to me. I shall preserve my word in everything and I shall make everything well."

Thus she echoes the Universalist message of St. Paul that God will be "all in all" (I Cor 15:28).

It is this Universality of God's love for *all* and God's presence in *all* that is the hallmark of all mystical religious experience whether or not theological statements of Universalism are proclaimed. As George Fox, founder of the Quaker movement, was known to repeat: "All creatures in God, and God in all creatures."

Mystical religious experiences are not limited to Christianity and are Universal, as expressed by the early 20th Century mystic and researcher Evelyn Underhill (Anglican): "This unmistakable experience has been achieved by the mystics of every religion; and when we read their statements, we know that all are speaking of the same thing." William James, the first American-born psychologist, believed that, "The founders of every church owed their power originally to the fact of their direct personal communication with the divine." If God loves us all, how could this be otherwise? This case for Universality has been well documented by other Christian writers, including John Hick (Universalist) who bases his Universalism in part on his own mystical experiences of God and Bruno Borchert (Carmelite priest).

Early Research

In studying the accounts of mystics from Biblical times to the present, it is easy to hear the recurring themes of 1) The continuity of God's love, and 2) The Oneness with God and the Universe. However, some of the first modern philosophers and theorists, lacking any objective data to support their views, dismissed religion as superstition and labeled mystics as having mental problems. The best example of this faulty reasoning is Sigmund Freud who pronounced that religious founders like Jesus were psychotic and that religious people were neurotic. Fortunately, at the time Freud was making unsupported claims (that would later be refuted), a champion arose to counter his flawed theories.

Over a hundred years ago, William James, the first American psychologist, began his serious study of religious experience. His classic work, *The Varieties of Religious Experience*, was published in 1901 but is still in print today. Using the basic tools of observation and case studies, he began to research religious visions and mystical experience. James was able to formulate some working hypotheses on the nature of religious experiences, and much of what he hypothesized has subsequently been tested in large-scale research projects that have usually validated his observations.

Modern Research

The big news today in the study of mystical religious experiences is sheer numbers! Social scientists now have documented thousands of people who have come forward to tell of their direct experience of God. Researchers can now state with absolute certainty that Freud was wrong—the number of people with personal experience of God is at least eight times greater than the number of people who have suffered psychotic episodes!

Large-scale surveys on mystical experience began in 1969 when Alister Hardy founded the Religious Experience Research Unit at Oxford University. In order to research mystical religious experience within the general population, Sir Hardy made an appeal to the general public via newspapers and pamphlets which asked the question, *"Have you ever been aware of or influenced by a presence or power, whether you call it 'God' or not, which is different from your everyday self?"* Readers were invited to send him their responses. Ten years later, Hardy published a book based on the first 3,000 responses he had received to this question. The Alister Hardy Religious Experience Research Center at Oxford also found that 95% of reported mystical experiences in their British national sample were positive.

The next significant step taken by social scientists to objectify research on this topic was in 1977 by David Hay and Ann Morisy. Using the same question about the experience of God used in the previous study, they studied a random sample of 1,865 British persons (rather than a self-selected group as in the first survey), and 35% responded "yes" to the question. Repeating the Alister Hardy question on mystical religious experience ten years later, a British Gallup Poll found that the number responding "yes" had risen to 48%. In Australia, a similar study the same year found 44% of the population reporting "yes" to the same question.

Between the appeal in the British newspaper for accounts and the objective large-scale population survey, Andrew Greely and his colleagues at the National Opinion Research Center at the University of Chicago began their surveying using a similar question: *"Have you ever felt as though you were very close to a powerful spiritual force that seemed to lift you out of yourself?"* A national sample of 1,467 Americans showed 39% responding "yes." Over the years, repeated national samples have shown that the number of people responding affirmatively to this question has varied from 35% to 50%. In a poll of Poles, Andrzej Kokoszka of the Copernicus School of Medicine in Krakow found that 54% of those surveyed reported at least one profoundly altered state of consciousness. These included 1) "Experience contact with a Divine Being or God" (36%) 2) "Experience of the impression that you understood everything, only it was impossible to utter this impression" (often called "cosmic consciousness") (28%), and 3) "Experience of the feeling of being One with the Universe" (16%).

Some evidence supports an increase in mystical experiences. Three in-depth British studies in which the respondents were interviewed rather than surveyed yielded positive response rates of over 60%. One-fourth of the respondents reported that they had never told anyone else of this experience for fear of being thought "mentally ill" or "stupid." When Americans were recently surveyed with the question: *"In general, how often would you say you had experienced God's presence or a spiritual force that felt very close to you?,"* an incredible 86% reported that this had happened to them one or more times!

Mystics Are Happier!

A survey of British by Hay and Morisy noted that people reporting mystical religious experiences tended to have greater psychological well-being than those who report no mystical religious experiences. In his survey of Americans, Andrew Greely noted the same phenomenon: "Mystics are happier." Ralph Hood has demonstrated a correlation between high scores on a scale of mystical experience and measures of mental health. Prof. Hay notes that studies on mysticism and mental health refute Sigmund Freud's hypothesis that religion was symptomatic of neurosis and religious experience was perhaps temporary psychosis. Hay further notes that studies in England, the United States, and Australia consistently show that mysticism is more apt to be reported by people in the upper-middle and professional middle classes rather than the lower classes. This disproves the Marxist hypothesis that religion is the "opiate of the masses." Also, the hypothesis of the sociologist Dirkheim that religious experience is typically an "effervescent group phenomenon," is refuted by a Gallup Poll survey in Britain in 1987 which found that 60% of accounts of religious experience occurred in the context of solitude.

Research into the mental health of those who have mystical experiences has shown mystical experiencers to be normal or healthy. My own feeling is that this may be due to the fact that it takes a certain amount of guts to come forward and tell others that you have been personally touched by God. This has become easier over the past forty years because research in the social sciences has documented that mystical experiences are common. Still, the tendency is for people not to come forward with mystical experiences unless they are sure that the people listening will accept them.

Differentiating from the Occult

People who engage in occult practices like to pretend their practices are mystic, but there is an easy test to determine the difference. The occult has to do with manipulating the paranormal for selfish personal ends such as influencing a person to become your lover, inflicting ill upon a person (as in the case of Voodoo dolls), or seeing the future with the intent of changing an outcome in your own favor. The most famous example of occult practices is found in the Book of 1st Samuel (I Sam 28:3-16) in which King Saul asks the medium of Endor to perform necromancy and conger up the spirit of the dead prophet Samuel in order to foresee the outcome of the next day's battle. In short, the occult is all about, "me, me, me!" *Mysticism is about God and from God.* Nothing evil ever comes from God (Jas 1:12-17). Whereas mystical experiences are positive and lead to happiness, psychologist Michael Argyle notes occult experiences have the opposite effect.

Research on Children

Interestingly, children's acknowledgment of the presence of God declines with age. When Finnish researcher Kalevi Tamminen asked children ages 7 to 20, *"Have you at times felt that God was particularly close to you?,* 84% of the first-graders acknowledged the presence of God. Curiously, by the end of high school, the number had declined to 47%. The modern world is often hostile to spirituality. There is also evidence that people may have mystical experiences but deny them. Carl Sagan, the famous physicist, once stated that he had felt on several occasions that his dead parents had tried to contact him, but he dismissed this as being impossible. He is unusual, as most people alter their beliefs when confronted with their own personal experience. On this topic, almost 40% of Americans report contact with the dead, according to the National Opinion Research Center.

Case Studies

Despite the incredible variety of human beings and human cultures, all true mystical religious experiences have an underlying similarity. Most importantly, mystics never "let go" of their experience, and it permanently alters their perspective on life. For those who know this experience personally, as well as for those who are gaining these insights vicariously, I wanted to present some of the powerfully moving accounts of mystical religious experiences expressed in the words of the mystics themselves. These cases give a greater insight into the experience itself as well as its effect on the individual.

I will begin with two of my own mystical religious experiences which were spontaneous. The first was one that is quite commonly reported. In fact, in a sermon some years ago, Rev. Horace Westwood described his own mystical experience that was virtually identical to this one of mine:

> It occurred in the winter of 1973 when I was 29 and a doctoral student in psychology at the University of Northern Colorado. Late one cold afternoon, I was in the parking lot with my back to the panorama of the Rocky Mountains, looking instead at a small dead tree in a snow bank. All at once, I was lifted up, and I was one with God and the Universe. I felt timeless and immortal. A few moments later, I was back to my normal state, but the moment has never left me. It left me knowing that we are all a part of God and that God is with us always.

Mystical experiences can happen at *any* time. St. Teresa had a mystical experience while cooking eggs for her convent—she reportedly burned the eggs! My second mystical experience occurred during my mid-forties while teaching at the University of Houston:

> I was at a football game in the Astrodome, waiting in the concession line. All at once, I felt as if I were inside the minds of all the people around me and that I could feel what they were feeling. I could feel their happiness, their love for their friends and family, and their joy at being together. Though it only lasted for a few moments, it was like tapping into the Spirit of God. I had often wondered what God gets out of Creation, and I got an answer that day: God gets to be all of us!

Mystical experiences vary widely from mild to overwhelming. Mine were definitely not of the magnitude of St. Paul or even Ralph Waldo Emerson, but I present them as examples of mild mystical experiences.

The following account is from a 56-year-old British female, one of the modern cases from Alister Hardy's Religious Experience Research Unit at Oxford University that appeared in his book, *The Spiritual Nature of Man*:

> On this occasion I found instead that I was overtaken by an intense feeling of affection for and unity with everyone around as they ran to catch buses, took children shopping, or joyfully met their friends. The feeling was so strong that I wanted to leave my silent vigil and join them in their urgent living.

This sense of 'Oneness' is basic to what I understand of religion. Hitherto I think I had only experienced it so irresistibly towards a few individuals—sometimes toward my children or when in love. The effect of the experience has been, I think, a permanent increase in my awareness that we are 'members one of another,' a consequent greater openness toward all and a widening of my concern for others.

The next account appeared in the 1937 edition of the Universalist magazine, *The Christian Leader* and is from author Mary Austin who had a mystical experience as a child:

> I must have been between 7 and 8, when this experience happened to me. It was a summer morning, and the child I was had walked down through the orchard alone and come out on the brow of a sloping hill where there was grass and the wind blowing and one tall tree reaching into the infinite immensities of blueness. Quite suddenly, after a moment of quietness there, earth and sky and tree and windblown grass and the child in the midst of them came alive together with a pulsing light of consciousness. There was a wild foxglove at the child's feet and a bee dozing about. And to this day, I recall the swift inclusive awareness of each for the whole—I in them, and they in me, and all of us enclosed in a warm, lucent bubble of livingness. I remember the child looking everywhere for the source of this happy wonder, and at last she questioned—'God'—because it was the only awesome word she knew. Deep inside like the murmurous swinging of a bell she heard the answer, 'God, God.' How long this ineffable moment lasted I never knew. It broke like a bubble at the sudden singing of a bird, and the wind blew and the world was the same as ever, only never quite the same.

Obviously, how people interpret their experience depends on their time and culture. Regarding my own mystical experiences, I freely admit that these experiences reinforced my belief that God communicates with human beings. I also interpret them in the same way as the great contemporary Universalist theologian, John Hick, who notes that he too has had mystical experiences that convinced him, "we know the Transcendent Holy Presence to be profoundly good to exist and in which the unknown future holds no possible threat."

The following are two mystical religious experiences of John Hick, the world's foremost Universalist/pluralist philosopher, extracted from his autobiography.

His first mystical experience (which was spontaneous) occurred at age 18 years while riding on the top deck of a bus:

> As everyone will be very conscious who can themselves remember such a moment, all descriptions are inadequate. But it was as though the skies opened up and light poured down and filled me with a sense of overflowing joy, in response to an immense transcendent goodness and love. I remember that I couldn't help smiling broadly—smiling back, as it were, at God—though if any of the other passengers were looking, they must have thought that I was a lunatic, grinning at nothing.

His next mystical experience was the "sought-after" variety and occurred many years later when Dr. Hick was practicing Buddhist meditation:

> I have once, but so far only once, experienced what was to me a startling breakthrough into a new form or level of consciousness. I was in that second stage and when eventually I opened my eyes the world was quite different in two ways. Whereas normally I am here, and the environment is there, separate from me, there was now no such distinction; and more importantly, the total universe of which I was part was friendly, benign, good, so that there could not possibly be anything to fear or worry about. It was a state of profound delight in being. This only lasted a short time, probably not more than two minutes.

The great 20th-Century mystical researcher, Evelyn Underhill, was herself a mystic. Early in her career, she described herself as a "passionate amateur of experience" and was very much interested in comparative religion. Later in her career, because of her mystical experiences, she identified herself primarily as a Christian, although she continued to be interested in world religion. The following mystical experience occurred to her in 1923 at the age of 48 years and is at the time of her centering on Christianity. This account is from Armstrong's biography of her:

> Such lights as one gets are now different in type: *all* overwhelming in their emotional result: quite independent 'sensible devotion', more quiet, calm, expansive, like intellectual intuitions yet not quite that either. Thus yesterday I saw and felt *how* it actually is, that we are in Christ and he is in us—the interpretation of the Spirit—and all of us merged together in him actually, and so fitly described as his body. The way to full intercessory power must, I think, be along this path.

The following is an account of a middle-aged female from Dr. Richard Bucke's *Cosmic Consciousness*:

> I was losing my consciousness, my identity, I was powerless to hold myself. Now came a period of rapture so intense that the Universe stood still, as if amazed at the unutterable majesty of the spectacle! Only one in all the infinite Universe! The All-loving, the Perfect One! The Perfect Wisdom, truth, love, and purity! And with the rapture came the insight. In that same wonderful moment of what might be called supernatural bliss, came illumination…What joy when I saw there was no break in the chain—not a link left out—everything in its time and place. Worlds, systems, all bended in one harmonious whole. Universal light, synonymous with Universal love!

In this account from *Cosmic Consciousness*, a 35 year old journalist, Paul Tyner, describes "the crowning experience of my life:"

> Now, indeed, it is plain, that being lifted up he shall lift all men with him—has lifted, is lifting and must ever continue to lift out of the very essence of his transcendent humanity. Immortality is no longer an hypothesis of the theologian, a figment of the imagination, a dream of the poet. Men shall live forever, because man, invincible to all effects of time and change, and even of murderous violence, lives today in the fullness of life and power that he enjoyed in his thirty-third year, with only added glory of goodness and greatness and beauty…This is the truth given age upon age to all men in all lands, and persistently misunderstood—the truth at last to be seen of all men in its fullness and purity.

Hannah Whitall Smith was a writer and the wife of a Quaker minister. In Chapter 22 of her book, *The Unselfishness of God and How I Discovered It*, she relates two mystical religious experiences of Universalism. Interestingly, some "Christian" publishers delete this chapter on Universalism. She writes:

> And with this a veil seemed to be withdrawn from before the plans of the universe, and I saw that it was true, as the *Bible* says, that 'as in Adam all die, even so in Christ should all be made alive.' As was the first, even so was the second. The 'all' in one case could not in fairness mean less than the 'all' in the other. I saw therefore that the remedy must necessarily be equal to the disease, the salvation must be as universal as the fall…God is the Creator of every human being, therefore He is the Father of each one, and they are all His children; and Christ died for every one, and is declared to be 'the propi-

tiation not for our sins only, but also for the sins of the whole world' (1 John 2:2). However great the ignorance therefore, or however grievous the sin, the promise of salvation is positive and without limitations…The how and the when I could not see; but the one essential fact was all I needed—somewhere and somehow God was going to make every thing right for all the creatures He had created. My heart was at rest about it forever.

This next account of a Universalist mystical experience is from Sir Hardy's *The Spiritual Nature of Man*, and describes Rev. Dr. Leslie Weatherhead's youthful experience:

> This is the only way I know in which to describe the moment, for there was nothing to see at all. I felt caught up into some tremendous sense of being within a loving, triumphant and shining purpose. I never felt more humble. I never felt more exalted. A most curious, but overwhelming sense possessed me and filled me with ecstasy. I felt that all was well for mankind—how poor the words seem! The word 'well' is so poverty stricken. All men were shining and glorious beings who in the end would enter incredible joy. Beauty, music, joy, love immeasurable and a glory unspeakable they would inherit. Of this they were heirs.

In this account from Prof. David Hay's *Exploring Inner Space*, a female writer recalls a mystical religious experience from childhood—an account that echoes an experience of the famous mystic Julian of Norwich:

> My father used to take all the family for a walk on Sunday evenings. On one such walk, we wandered across a narrow path through a field of high, ripe corn. I lagged behind, and found myself alone. Suddenly, heaven blazed upon me. I was enveloped in golden light, I was conscious of a presence, so kind, so loving, so bright, so consoling, so commanding, existing apart from me but so close. I heard no sound. But words fell into my mind quite clearly—'Everything is all right. Everybody will be all right.'

The following account is that of Richard Bucke, a Canadian neuropsychiatrist and scholar of comparative religion whose mystical religious experience inspired him to research and write *Cosmic Consciousness*:

> All at once, without warning of any kind, I found myself wrapped in a flame-colored cloud. For an instant I thought of fire, an immense conflagration somewhere close by in that great city; the next, I knew that the fire was within myself. Directly afterward there came upon me a sense of exultation,

of immense joyousness accompanied or immediately followed by an intellectual illumination impossible to describe. Among other things, I did not merely come to believe, but I saw that the universe is not composed of dead matter, but is, on the contrary, a living Presence; I became conscious in myself of eternal life. It was not a conviction that I would have eternal life, but a consciousness that I possessed eternal life then; I saw that all men are immortal; that the cosmic order is such that without any peradventure all things work together for the good of each and all; that the foundation principle of the world, of all the worlds, is what we call love, and that the happiness of each and all is in the long run absolutely certain. The vision lasted a few seconds and was gone; but the memory of it and the sense of the reality of what it taught has remained during the quarter of a century which has since elapsed. I knew that what the vision showed was true. I had attained to a point of view from which I saw that it must be true. That view, that conviction, I may say that consciousness, has never, even during periods of the deepest depression, been lost.

The following is an account of a 55-year-old male taken from Prof. Timothy Beardsworth's *A Sense of Presence*:

> One lunch time I had been helping to dry dishes after the meal, and was standing before the open drawer of the sideboard putting knives and forks away. I was not thinking of anything, apart from vague attention to the job I was doing. Suddenly, without warning, I was flooded with the most intense blue-white light I have ever seen. Words can never adequately nor remotely touch the depth of this experience. It was like looking into the face of the sun, magnified several times in its light-intensity. It would be truer to say that I lost all sense of self in a total immersion in Light. But more 'real' than the Light itself was the unbearable ecstasy that accompanied it. All sense of time or self disappeared, yet it could only have been a fraction of a second. I knew only a sense of infinite dimension, and a knowledge that this was the Spirit of God Almighty, which was the hidden Life-Light-Love in all men, all life and all creation. I knew that nothing existed apart from this Spirit. It was infinite Love, Peace, Law, Power, Creation and the Ultimate Truth and Perfection. It was all Wisdom, Tolerance, Understanding and Eternal Life for all people. I also knew that had I been suffering from any so-called incurable disease whatsoever, I would have become instantly whole. Then after the fraction of a second—I became myself again, still standing beside the open drawer putting knives and forks away. That one moment was and

remains the most vital moment of my life, for there has never been a repetition. But out of it was born the Mission to which I have for many years dedicated my life…

Summary

Regarding mystical religious experiences, it is valid to say that 1) They happen to a large percent of the population, 2) The overwhelming majority of those people are normal, healthy, and no more apt to be mentally ill than the general population, and 3) They change people's lives.

Modern accounts assure us that truly God is with us always, and that in time, "All flesh shall see the salvation of God" (Lk 3:6). Until then, the *Bible* can be our source for accessing the Holy Spirit promised to us by Jesus, and Jesus' teachings instruct us in the way to build the Kingdom of God within our midst. Testimony of those in the *Bible* and that of the mystics assure us all that God is there for *all* of us, and mystical religious experiences serve as a continuing reminder of the loving presence of God in our lives.

The Spirit of God has been and is with us always.

There is no doubt we live in God.

Amen

All references cited in the text are listed in the reference section for the entire book.

8

The Near-Death Experience and Christian Universalism

(**Note:** This chapter is based on an article first published in the *Journal of Near-Death Studies,* 22 (1), Fall 2003, 57-71.)

Of all the theological explanations for the near-death experience, the Doctrine of Universal Salvation (a.k.a., Universalism) is the most obvious "fit." Universalism embraces the idea that God is too good to condemn humankind to Eternal Hell and that—sooner or later—*all* humanity will be saved. Interestingly, a belief in Universal Salvation can be found in virtually all the world's major religions. It is particularly essential to Zoroastrianism, the religion of the Magi.

The Universalist theology that acknowledges a temporary Hellish state for those who need some "shaping up" before proceeding to their ultimate reward is termed more specifically, "Restorative Universalism." In my book, *Visions of God from the Near-Death Experience,* I included a chapter on the "negative" near-death experience, coupled with Hell as portrayed in sacred scriptures. My intention then was to present the topic of Universal Salvation in the world's religions from a spiritual perspective. In this chapter, I want to show that Christian Universalism—a doctrine with solid support in the *New Testament*—blends seamlessly with the experience of the near-death experience.

I hope to offer a source of comfort not only to the general reader, but also specifically to near-death experiencers, both Christian and non-Christian, who may have had their experience marginalized by assaults from Fundamentalist or Conservative Christians. They can be assured that a more loving alternative to Christian "exclusivity" (i.e., "only Christians go to Heaven") exists within the same *New Testament* they have known since childhood.

In a recent national poll for *Religion & Ethics Newsweekly* and *U. S. News & World Report* only 19% of Christians and 7% of non-Christians stated a belief that their religion is the only true religion. This contrasts with a 1965 poll by sociologists, Glock and Stark, in which 65% of Protestants and 51% of Catholics reported that, "belief in Jesus Christ as Savior was absolutely necessary for Salvation."

Americans appear to be becoming more Universalist in their orientation. The 2002 study also found that, "an individual's spiritual experience (as opposed to doctrines and beliefs) is the most important part of religion" was answered in the affirmative by 69% of Christians and 73% of non-Christians. Americans also appear to be more spiritually aware or, at least, we are more willing to admit it. In 2002, 86% of Americans stated that they had, "experienced God's presence or a spiritual force that felt very close to you one or more times."

While spirituality has always been part of religious experience, how are Universalist ideas expressed in the *Bible*? More importantly, how does Universalism help us place the near-death experience within the context of Christian theology?

Validity of the *Bible*

To answer these questions, we must first consider the status of the *Bible* and theological interpretations of it. In recent polls regarding the validity of the *Bible*, about one-third of Americans reported a belief that the *Bible* is "the actual Word of God" (about as many as report being Fundamentalist). One-sixth (about the number of non-Christians in America) described it as a "book of fables, legends, history, and moral precepts." One-half believed it to be the "inspired Word of God but that not everything should be taken literally." These views of the general population reflect modern scholarship regarding the *Bible*. Today, Biblical inerrancy is a view adhered to by only the most Fundamentalist scholars.

The *Bible* contains a treasure-trove of ancient accounts of mystical religious experiences. Conservative Christian scholar, Luke Timothy Johnson, correctly notes that what is ignored in modern studies of Christian origins are the mystical religious experiences so clearly described in the *New Testament*. Moderate Christian scholar James D. G. Dunn notes in referring to Jesus that, "there is no incidence of a healing miracle that falls clearly outside the general character of psycho-somatic illness." Nevertheless, his book is a study on what may be called "communicative theism"—the direct contact between God and humanity in the *New Testament*. Even the liberal Jesus Seminar voiced no doubt that Jesus appeared to some of his followers after his death.

Scholars of religious experience note that since the time the *Bible* was written to the present, individuals have reported mystical experiences. The near-death experience is unique among the categories of mystical union with God because of its identifiable "trigger." The big question is: How much credibility should one give to reports of mystical experiences in the *Bible*, as most are not first-person accounts but rather written down as "much-told" tales following many years of oral tradition?

As stated before, most modern scholars do not consider the *Bible* to be inerrant. In light of this, it becomes untenable in theological interpretation to base your theological program on one or two *Bible* verses. For example, the basis of papal authority is inferred from two verses in the Gospel of Matthew (Matt 16:18-19). Even more difficult is justification for the Trinity which is not in the *Bible* and can at best only be inferred by the fact that God, God's Spirit, and Jesus are mentioned together in two verses (Matt 28:19, II Cor 13:14). I will discuss more about how theology can be based on a preponderance of verses in the *New Testament* later in this article.

Christian Universalism

Universalism as a theological system traces its history back to Origen (185-254 CE). The Universalist Church in North America was, for a time during the 19th Century, the sixth largest denomination in the United States. The Universalist Church merged with the Unitarians in 1961, and Unitarian Universalist Christians still make up a majority of members world-wide. In the United States, it has developed into an inter-faith church in which Unitarian Universalist Christians comprise only a minority.

As stated earlier, there are several variants on Christian Universalism. Some Universalists believe that God will save you, "no matter what." This is a variant on "Jesus Saves" theology, except that "Jesus Saves Everybody" by his atoning sacrifice. Another variant is the belief that Christians will be saved immediately, and all others will be saved after becoming believers. Restorative Universalism assumes a judgment ("Life Review" in near-death experience terminology) and punishment for some, followed by Universal Salvation for *all*.

Today, most Christians who profess a belief in Universal Salvation belong to a variety of other denominations. One of the most important things I have learned during my years of working with the Foundation for Contemporary Theology in Houston is that, despite their questions about doctrine, most Liberal Christians choose to remain within more mainline denominations, most often for reasons of tradition. Examples of prominent contemporary Universalist Christian theologians in other denominations are Jan Bonda (Dutch Reformed) Tom Harpur (Anglican), John Hick (United Reformed Church), and Thomas Talbott (Independent Christian).

It is noteworthy that, in addition to being a Christian scholar, Tom Harpur is a Near-Death researcher, and he includes a strong Universalist Christian statement at the end of his book, *Life after Death*. One can also find Universalist Christianity and the near-death experience discussed on the internet.

Christian theologies are systems created to explain the diverse and conflicting accounts given by the various authors of the *New Testament*. Often theologians will arrive at differing interpretations of what the words in a particular *Bible* verse mean. For example, **"I am the way, and the truth, and the life. No one comes to the Father except through me"** (John 14:6) is a primary verse used by "Jesus Saves" theologians; however, this verse has been interpreted by Liberal Christians such as Marcus Borg as meaning that salvation comes from following the teachings of Jesus rather than from some formula of belief.

In an article in *Christianity Today* entitled, "The Gift of Salvation," Timothy George makes a case for "Jesus Saves" theology by citing just 23 verses from the *New Testament*. By my own calculations, there were 139 verses supporting "Jesus Saves" theology, 551 verses supporting Salvation by Good Works (with 389 of its 551 verses on the lips of Jesus himself; see *Appendix A*), and 273 verses supporting Universal Salvation (including the 42 verses which speak to Hell not being permanent; see *Appendix B*) in the *New Testament*. It is worth noting that a fourth theological position, the Doctrine of Predestination, has 77 verses to support it with 55 coming from the *New Testament*. One can see from the sheer magnitude of data that Salvation by Good Works has the most support, followed by Universal Salvation for *all*. The two taken together form the case for Christian Restorative Universalism.

Universalism and the Near-Death Experience

When it comes to the near-death experience, Universalism is the most logical theological "fit." Why? Let us explore some basics of Christian Restorative Universalism and the near-death experience. Near-death experiences often begin with an "out of body" experience (OBE). The *Bible* records this 2,000-year-old OBE by St. Paul:

> I know a person in Christ who fourteen years ago was caught up to the third Heaven—whether in the body or out of the body I do not know; God knows. And I know that such a person—whether in the body or out of the body I do not know; God knows—was caught up into Paradise and heard things that were not to be told, that no moral is permitted to repeat (II Cor 12:2-5).

One of the most reported characteristics of an in-depth near-death experience is the experience of Light or Being of Light. Some near-death experiencers feel that this Light represents God or God's emissary, as in the following:

> I was in the Universe and I was Light. It takes all the fear of dying out of you. It was Heavenly. I was in the Presence of God.

> I went directly into the Light, and my pain ceased. There was a feeling of extreme peace.

In the *Bible*, we read:

> God is light, and in him there is no darkness at all (1 Jn 1:5). Every generous act of giving, with every perfect gift, is from above, coming down from the Father of lights (Jas 1:17)....he who is the blessed and only Sovereign, the King of kings and Lord of lords. It is he alone who has immortality and dwells in unapproachable light...(1 Tim 6:15-16).

Near-death experiencers routinely report an immense amount of unconditional love radiating from the Being of Light.

> An absolute white Light that is God—all loving. The unification of us with our Creator.

> I left my body, and I was surrounded by God. It didn't feel male or female, young or old, just me. I was surrounded by Love...I looked down at the little girl in bed...later when I realized it was me, I was back in my body.

In the *Bible*, we read:

> Beloved, let us love one another, because love is from God; everyone who loves is born of God and knows God. Whoever does not love does not know God, for God is love (I Jn 4:7-8). The steadfast love of the Lord never ceases, his mercies never come to an end (Lam 3:22).

Near-death experiencers report a feeling of "Oneness with God" and a sensation of being "In God."

> And deep within me came an instant and wondrous recognition: I, even I, was facing God.

> It is something which becomes you and you become it. I could say, "I was peace; I was love." It was the brightness...it was part of me.

In the *Bible*, we read:

> For in him we live and move and have our being (Acts 17:28). For from him and through him and to him are all things (Rom 11:36). One God and Father of all, who is above all and through all and in all (Eph 4:6).

Sometimes near-death experiencers encounter Jesus in the Light.

> The light was in me and between the molecules, the cells in my body. He was in me—I was in him…I knew all things. I saw all things. I was all things. But not me; Jesus had this. As long as I was "in Him," and he was "in me," I had this power, this glory (for lack of a better word).

> I left but stood there wanting to help this poor soul (which was in effect me). Then I was on the third level and a voice said, "choose." I saw Jesus, the Blessed Mother, and the archangel Michael. My message was unconditional love; learn to love your family; you love others, but learn to love your family.

These accounts recall the Apostle Paul's experience of Jesus. Many scholars consider his account in I Corinthians 15:5-8 as the only first-hand account of the resurrection of Jesus. Paul also provides verified second-hand accounts of Jesus' appearance to Peter and James. In Acts, we have a description of Paul's experience of Jesus.

> Now as he was going along and approaching Damascus, suddenly a light from Heaven flashed around him. He fell to the ground and heard a voice saying, "Saul, Saul, why do you persecute me?" (Acts 9:3-4; also 22:6-7; 26:12-14)

Researcher Philip Wiebe maintains that there is no difference between modern-day visions of Jesus and similar visions of Jesus described in the *Bible*. While Professor Wiebe excluded near-death experiences from his research, numerous near-death experience accounts over the past quarter century attest to face-to-face meetings with Jesus. Interestingly both Prof. Wiebe and Dr. Barbara Rommer note in their books that even people of religions other than Christianity have described encounters with Jesus.

Before turning our attention from the Light, it is worth noting that Fundamentalists often counter this common near-death experience phenomenon with a verse from St. Paul: "Even Satan disguises himself as a being of Light" (II Cor 11:14). This is invalid for two reasons: 1) It places too much weight on a single *Bible* verse, and 2) The overwhelming amount of data leaves no doubt that the

Light experienced by the near-death experiencer radiates *love*. Jesus tells us how to distinguish false prophets: **"You will know them by their fruits"** (Matt 7:16). When Jesus himself was accused of being Satanic, he explained:

> **And the scribes who came down from Jerusalem said, "He has Beelzebub and by the ruler of the demons he casts out demons." And he called to them and spoke to them in parables, "How can Satan cast out Satan? If a kingdom is divided against itself, that kingdom cannot stand. And if a house is divided against itself, that house will not be able to stand. And if Satan has risen up against himself and is divided, he cannot stand, but his end is come"** (Mk 3:22-26).

Fundamentalist Christians cannot have it both ways. The Light cannot represent goodness for a Christian and deception for non-Christians. Satan may be a neon sign, but God is the Light of the Universe.

Jesus tells us that God is our Father too.

> **I am ascending to my Father and your Father, to my God and your God** (Jn 20:17).

> **You have one Father—the one in heaven** (Matt 23:9).

We also read in the *Bible*:

> 'I will be your Father and you shall be my Sons and Daughters,' says the Lord Almighty (II Cor 6:18).

> **Is there anyone among you who, if your child asks for bread, would give him a stone? Or if the child asks for a fish, would give a snake? If you then who are evil, know how to give good gifts to your children, how much more will your Father in Heaven give good things to those who ask Him?** (Matt 7:9-10)

What kind of parent abandons his or her child? Surely not the loving God Jesus talked about!

Judgment/Life Review

Judgment in near-death experience terminology is called, "Life Review." This is usually a positive experience.

> I found myself in a corridor. The corridor did not end. I was not afraid. There was a white light. Very clear white colors of light. Off to the side, I

could see shades of gray. Off to the side, I could see my childhood passing, going left to right. I thought to myself, "I am getting younger." I did not see my adult life. I felt like I was not alone, but I did not see anybody.

During the Judgment [it was] like on a Rolodex. I could feel the person by me. I was waiting for the bad to come up, but nothing bad was coming up.

For others, there is a perception of one's effect on other people.

I saw this life "pass in front of my eyes," like watching a movie. I felt others' pain, joy, sorrows.

For some, life review is a negative experience:

It was not peaceful, much baggage, much unfinished business. All things are connected. You are not your body, you are a soul; mine was in limbo. I knew I would be in limbo for a long time. I had a life review and was sent to the void.

Comparative religion scholar Farnaz Masumain notes that in Christianity, sometimes God is seen as Judge of the World, but more often, Jesus is seen as the Judge. In Jesus' parable of the Rich Man and Lazarus (Lk 16:19-31), he states that judgment began prior to him, is ongoing, and occurs immediately after death. In the Judgment of the Nations (Matt 25:31-46), Jesus is Judge of the entire world—both Christian and non-Christian. Judgment is based on good works done to the **"least of these"** (Matt 25:40).

Jesus taught that we must be judged but that God is Light and goodness:

God is light, and in Him there is no darkness at all (1 Jn 1:5).

Near-death experiencers often note that the Being of Light in the Life Review offers total acceptance.

My near-death experience was before Moody's book came out. When it did, I said, "Oh my God! Mine is pretty classic—just like the book." It was incredibly clear—my life—going through what happened. There were figures around I did not know. The white Light was wonderful! It was just love. I knew my life would be reviewed. It was like flipping pages. I knew I had done things I was not proud of, but there was total acceptance. I wanted to stay, but I was told to go back and be loving.

I have already noted above that this is also true when the Being of Light is specifically identified as Jesus. This is the picture that the *New Testament* presents of Jesus. In the mystic Gospel of John we read:

You judge by human standards. I judge no one (Jn 8:15).

And I, when I am lifted up from the Earth, will draw all people to myself (Jn 12:3).

Jesus teaches us:

My yoke is easy, and my burden is light (Matt 11:30).

The following makes it clear that Jesus is an advocate for both Christians and non-Christians:

> My children, I am writing these things to you so that you may not sin. But if anyone does sin, we have an advocate with the Father; Jesus Christ the Righteous. He is the atoning sacrifice for our sins, and not for ours only, but also for the sins of the whole world (I Jn 2:2).

With Jesus as Judge, no one is ever abandoned—Christian or non-Christian. Jesus tells us that the Kingdom of God is not only for the pure (Matt 5:8) but also for the impure (Matt 15:2, 21-31; Lk 18:10-14), the pagan (Matt 15:21-28), and the heretic (Lk 10:25-37; Jn 4:16-30).

Near-death experiencers often feel that they judge themselves, as these three brief examples indicate:

> You are judging yourself. You have been forgiven all your sins, but are you able to forgive yourself for not doing the things you should have done and some little cheaty things that maybe you've done in your life? This is the judgment.

> I didn't see anyone as actually judging me. It was more like I was judging myself on what I did and how that affected everyone.

> I told the Light that...I expected him to judge me rather sternly. He said, "Oh, no, that doesn't happen at all." However, at my request, they then played back over the events that occurred in my life...and I was the judge.

Jesus clearly tells us:

Do not judge, so that you may not be judged. For with the judgment you make you will be judged, and the measure you give will be the measure you get (Matt 7:1-2).

The judgment of Jesus is not based on belief in Doctrine. The test is not about correct belief, but good deeds (see *Appendix A*).

Not everyone who says to me, 'Lord, Lord,' will enter the Kingdom of Heaven, but only the one who does the will of my Father in Heaven (Matt 7:21).

Good deeds will be rewarded:

For the Son of Man is to come with his angels in the glory of his Father, and then he will repay everyone for what has been done (Matt 16:27).

St. Peter reiterates:

I truly understand that God shows no partiality, but in every nation, anyone who fears him and does what is right is acceptable to Him (Acts 10:34-35).

St. Paul says:

For he will repay according to each one's deeds (Rom 2:6).

For God shows no partiality (Rom 2:11).

St. John of Patmos wrote,

And the dead were judged according to their works as recorded in the books (Rev 20:12).

Hell Is Not Permanent

The experience of Hell has been recorded in the near-death experience since the beginning of modern research. In near-death experience terminology, these are called "unpleasant" near-death experiences. In religious terms, the place of punishment is called variously "Hell," "Hades," "Limbo," "Purgatory," "Gehenna," and "Eternal Punishment." Modern-day near-death researchers have about as many categories of Hell as the ancient and medieval authors. Often in the near-death experience, accounts of Hell are not permanent (see *Appendix B*).

> I was in Hell...I cried up to God, and it was by the power of God and the mercy of God that I was permitted to come back.

> God, I am not ready, please help me...I remember when I screamed (this) an arm shot out of the sky and grabbed my hand and at the last second I was kept from falling off the end of the funnel, the lights flashing; and the heat was really something.

If Hell is not permanent (*see Appendix B*), one might wonder why Jesus says the "goats" will endure "eternal punishment" (Matt 25:46). Like virtually every Universalist scholar before him, Prof. Thomas Talbott notes that the Greek word for "forever" is better understood as "that which pertains to an age." For example, when Jonah was swallowed by the great fish, he "went down to the land whose bars closed on me forever" (Jonah 2:6). However, the story ends when Jonah is released by God from his bondage after just three days. In three other instances—his parable of the unforgiving servant (Matt 18:34-35) and his descriptions of a prisoner's fate (Matt 5:25-26, Lk 12:59)—Jesus indicates that punishment is not eternal but lasts only until your entire debt is paid (Matt 18:34). The following are classic passages supporting Christian Universalism:

> For Christ also suffered for sins once and for all, the righteous for the unrighteous, in order to bring you to God. He was put to death in the flesh, but made alive in the Spirit in which also he went and made a proclamation to the spirits in prison, who in former times did not obey (I Pet 2:18-20). For this reason the Gospel was proclaimed even to the dead, so that though they had been judged in the flesh as everyone is, they might live in the Spirit as God does (I Pet 4:6).

It appears from near-death experience accounts that Jesus is still rescuing people from Hell!

Universal Salvation

In the end, we will all be united with God (*see Appendix B*). The following is a sample of verses supporting Christian Universalism. Two of Jesus' most poignant parables proclaim Universal Salvation. In Matthew, God (the Good Shepherd) seeks and saves the lost sheep; the sheep does not return to the flock of its own accord. The parable ends, **"So it is not the will of your Father in Heaven that**

one of these little ones should be lost" (Matt 18:14). In the story of the Prodigal Son (Lk 15:11-32), the returning son does not ask to be a member of the family but for a job as his father's servant. It is God (the father) who takes him back into the family. The father is the character with the active role. People often have difficulty with this story because they wrongly identify with the good son and not with the father. Considering how much human parents love their children, the story puts some perspective on how much God, who is all good, loves each of us. From the mystic Gospel of John:

> **I have other sheep that do not belong to this fold, and I must bring them also, and they will listen to my voice. So there will be one flock, one shepherd** (Jn 10:16).
>
> **And I, when I am lifted up from the earth, will draw all people to myself** (Jn 12:32).

Universal salvation is reiterated in numerous writings of the other Apostles:

> When all things are subjected to him then the Son himself will also be subjected to the one who put all things in subjection under him, so that God may be all in all (1 Cor 15:28).
>
> For to this end we toil and struggle, because we have our hope set on the living God, who is the Savior of all people, especially of those who believe (1 Tim 4:10).
>
> And the Holy Spirit also testifies to us, for after saying, "This is the covenant I will make with them after those days, says the Lord: I will put my laws in their hearts and I will write them on their minds," he also adds: "I will remember their sins and their lawless deeds no more." Where there is forgiveness of these, there is no longer any offering for sin (Heb 10:15-17).
>
> He has made known to us the mystery of his will, according to his good pleasure that he set forth in Christ, as a plan for the fullness of time, to gather up all things in him, things in heaven and things on earth (Eph 1:9-10).
>
> For the grace of God has appeared, bringing salvation to all (Titus 2:11).

After-Effects

Dr. Bruce Greyson notes that one of the most lasting parts of the near-death experience is its after-effects. Experiences of God change and affirm lives, and sometimes this represents a "soft" change.

> It took some time for me to realize I was consumed with an insatiable thirst for knowledge. Dr. Pat Fenske wrote in the June, 1991, *Vital Signs* newsletter that individuals shift to a higher level of consciousness. I can relate to this 100%, and this has enabled me to understand why I look at things from an entirely different perspective from most people.
>
> Why did this experience change me so greatly? Why am I convinced that this was the most real thing that ever happened to me when logic and common sense dictate it wasn't? Why so many unexplained events since then…? The experience left me a changed person but not knowing why, full of questions and still seeking answers.

In some cases, the changes following an near-death experience are dramatic—as life-changing as St. Paul's mystical religious vision of Jesus that transformed him from a persecutor of Christians to an Evangelist for Jesus (I Cor 15:3-8; Gal 1:13-16). That kind of powerful effect occurred in the life of art professor Howard Storm who, after his encounter with Jesus during his near-death experience, abandoned his atheism and became a Christian minister. Rev. Storm related that when he began to pray, his near-death experience changed from a Hellish experience to a positive, loving one. He said, "Simply stated, I knew God loved me."

Summary

Like near-death experiences, death-bed visions and post-death visions point to an afterlife. But near-death experiences, like mystical religious experiences throughout the ages, are especially rich in insights into the nature of God. Near-death experiences, like other mystical religious experiences, both compliment and continue the testimony of that great repository of Western mystical experience, the *Bible*.

God's love is greater than we imagine or than we can imagine—this is the testimony of the Prophets, Sages, Saints, Mystics, and ordinary people throughout the ages who have shared with us their incomparable sense of Oneness with God and God's unconditional love for us *all*. Truly God is with us always and, in time, "All flesh shall see the salvation of God" (Lk 3:6).

All references cited in the text are listed in the notes and reference section for the entire book.

9

"All Flesh Shall See the Salvation of God"

The *Golden Thread* of Universalism can be found throughout the *Bible* and offers a view of Salvation consistent with the teachings of Jesus. Universal Salvation is so appealing because of what it says about God—that God is a loving parent who promises reconciliation for *all*—and what it says about the people who cannot imagine God any other way. As shown in the previous chapters, Universal Restoration is supported by a significant number of *Bible* verses.

As soon as Christianity split from Judaism, Christians began a long history of fracturing into groups—each with its own convictions about who Jesus was and what meaning to give to his life on Earth. Later, reformers arose to challenge these views and develop new ones as their experience of God changed. Over the years, people of God argued about every theological question, especially the requirements for acceptance into Heaven! Since the *Bible* itself included more than one formula—Good Works, Universal Salvation, "Belief" in Jesus, Predestination, Mysticism—how was one to determine which was "truer" than the others?

God's Exclusive Club?

Many Christians adopted a belief that only Christians went to Heaven. Others narrowed the "saved" to include only their own denomination or branch of Christianity. In their view, those who departed from their singular doctrinal interpretation were relegated to Eternal Hell. This "exclusive" interpretation was (and is) usually based on verses like John 3:16 (**"For God so loved the world that he gave his only Son, so that everyone who believes in him may not perish but may have eternal life."**).

Remember always that there are many ways to interpret the *Bible*, and this verse is no exception! An equally valid alternative understanding of John 3:16 is that Jesus declares early Christians blessed for believing in his message. Some Universalists use John 3:16 as a prelude to the verses that proclaim Jesus as Savior of *all*. Interestingly, the Universalist theologian Randy Klassen cites data which indicates that people who base their salvation on "belief" in Jesus alone (as opposed to belief that leads to good works) usually discontinue their church participation within just 6-8 weeks.

Virtually all religions promise a special place in the afterlife for their followers. If Jesus only saves those who love him, what good is that? Does not Lord Krishna promise to do the same? But Jesus calls us to a higher level—God's level. When Jesus tells us to love our enemies (Matt 5:44), is he asking us to be better than God? No, he is asking us to be like God, **"for he makes the sun to rise on the evil and on the good, and sends rain on the righteous and the unrighteous"** (Matt 5:45).

God Predestines All

A few verses in the *Bible* have been interpreted as meaning that God has predetermined a "quota" of persons for salvation. In fact, there are many more verses that favor Universal Restoration than predestination (see Appendix A, B, &C). Universalists contend that if predestination exists, God predestined *all* to be saved!

Double Bonus for Good Works!

The most basic teaching of Jesus in the Synoptic Gospels of Matthew, Mark, and Luke is the necessity for good works. Jesus constantly tries to persuade his listeners that being religious involves more than not being "bad" or adhering obsessively to prescribed rules, rites, and rituals. We must actively *do good* while in this world. We earn a double bonus when we do something beneficial for humankind: the satisfaction we feel in making the world better in the immediate here-and-now *and* the eventual reward of the Hereafter! Jesus made it clear that our actions toward others were paramount in determining how we will be judged: **"Do not judge, so that you may not be judged"** (Matt 7:1), **"For if you forgive others their trespasses, your heavenly Father will also forgive you"** (Matt 6:14), and **"In everything do to others as you would have them do to you"** (Matt 7:12). By leading good lives, we hasten the time of purification and Universal Restoration (II Pet 3:11-13). In Acts, Peter says, "Repent therefore, and turn to God so that your sins may be wiped out, so that times of refreshing may come from the presence of the Lord, and that he may send the Messiah appointed for you, that is, Jesus, who must remain in heaven until the time of *universal res-*

toration that God announced long ago through his holy prophets (Acts 3:19-21, *emphasis added*).

Universalism—None Are Left Out

Universalism acknowledges God's love for *all*. It asserts that God has always been there for us. God is the Ultimate good parent who has never abandoned us and will never abandon us. We humans can become estranged from God, but God is never estranged from humans. God is the parent of us *all* (Matt 23:9; Jn 20:17; II Cor 6:18), and in the end, God will save us *all* (Titus 2:11).

Jesus instructs us to love both our neighbors *and* our enemies (Matt 5:43-45)! If such extraordinary love for *all* others is required of us, then surely God's capacity for love is far more magnanimous and not limited to members of an exclusive club or a predestined few! The idea that we are expected to be better than God is unthinkable.

Universalists Differ on the Details

Universalism has been an enduring (although a minority) theological position since the early days of Christianity. But even Universalists have not been immune from internal disputes about specific details. For instance, Universalists have argued whether purification is instantaneous at the time of death or whether souls spend some time in Hell. Does God determine how long a soul spends in Hell or is it up to the individual to abandon his/her self-absorption and turn to God? Are the doors of Hell locked from the inside? Roman Catholic Universalists Dennis, Sheila, and Matthew Linn see free will as supreme and Universal Salvation as a result of God's overpowering love which will draw all souls to God.

Salvation in Other Religions?

Modern Universalists also disagree on whether *all* are saved by Jesus alone or whether other religions also know the way to God. The Universalist theologian John Hick notes that Vatican II declared that Christ died for *all* and that grace works in *all* human good will. This position has been re-iterated by John Paul II who in 1979 wrote, "Every man has been redeemed by Christ...Christ is in a way united even when man is unaware of it." This is essentially the position of modern Universalist theologians like Dennis, Sheila, and Matthew Linn (Roman Catholic), Jan Bonda (Dutch Reformed), and Thomas Talbott (independent).

Many Universalists today maintain that other faiths also know the Way to God. It is widely accepted that all modern religions teach the importance of good works and have some version of "The Golden Rule." Modern Universalist theologians John Hick (United Reformed) and Tom Harpur (Anglican), profess this view. I am also convinced that other valid pathways to God exist based mainly on my understanding of the nature of God, but also on the interfaith experiences and interfaith friendships over my lifetime. A strong undercurrent of Universalist thought pervades both of my previous religious books.

In *The Magi: From Zoroaster to the "Three Wise Men"*, I compare the religion of the Magi (Zoroastrianism) to Christianity and show the parallels of Universal Restoration in both faiths. While the majority of scholars throughout history have identified the Magi at the birth of Jesus as Zoroastrian priests, almost all have overlooked the fact that Zoroaster predicted the coming of future "Saviors" from countries other than Persia (Yasna 34.13). The Magi were most likely familiar with the Jewish expectation of a savior (Dan 7:13-14), since the two religions had been intermingling ever since the Magian King Cyrus the Great had freed the Jews from Babylonian captivity (Ezra 1:2-10). To me, the Magi at the birth of Jesus (Matt 2:1-12) represent the Greatest Interfaith Meeting in history! Also, Zoroaster was a Universalist. In his hymn to God, he states:

> If you understand these laws of happiness and pain
> Which Mazda (God) has ordained, O mortal men,
> (There is) a long period of punishment for the wicked
> And reward for the pious
> *But threreafter eternal joy shall reign forever* (Yasna 30.1, *emphasis added*).

In *Visions of God from the Near-Death Experience*, the wisdom of the prophets and sages of the world's religions is superimposed upon the accounts of modern near-death experiencers to illustrate the similarities between them. Persons from different cultures and religions describe the same feeling of overwhelming, unconditional love of God. Those whose experience was initially Hellish often report a reversal after calling out to God or calling out to Jesus. While researching the book, I talked with several people who said they had gone to Hell—some who had been rescued and some who had not. Although most near-death experiencers are dead technically only a few minutes before being revived, those who had experienced Hell recalled that the duration of their time there seemed considerably longer! In addition, few who had suffered through the experience of Hell chose to describe it by some "nicer," less negative name (like Hades, Purgatory, etc.)! God appears to be able to rehabilitate people quickly, but how long people spend in Hell is known only to God. As the 19th Century Universalist Hosea Ballou noted, it doesn't make sense that God would punish humans an

Eternity for things done during their brief lifespan. After his death, Jesus went to Hell to rescue the disobedient (I Pet 3:18-20; 4:6), and near-death experiencers tell us that they are still being rescued today. In my mind, the near-death experience is an expression of Universal Restoration.

In the West, despite all the changes in our culture, Jesus remains our primary path to God. Jesus adds to our knowledge of God's love and tells us that it is not our job to judge others. Only God knows the assets and limitations of our hearts. No matter which details regarding God's Universalism are correct, the *Bible* presents an undisputable message of Universal Salvation and Universal Restoration in the end. God is infinitely better than the best person you know (Matt 5:45; 6:25-32), and God wants everybody to be saved (I Tim 2:3-4). If God wills it, does anyone doubt it will happen?

If those who practice other faiths go to Heaven, should Christians evangelize? I think the answer is, "Yes!" Jesus' message of God's love and how to live in the Kingdom of God right now need to be brought to all who remain in darkness. Those who preach hate and fear instead of love are in darkness and practice evil religion. Although we'd prefer to think that "evil" always lies in other religions and not our own, thoughtful reflection forces us to acknowledge a shameful history of evil in the past nurtured by Christian exclusivity—the Crusades, witch hunts, and the Holocaust. The best evangelism is by example. In the words of Jesus, **"Let your light shine before others, so that they may see your good works and give glory to your Father in Heaven"** (Matt 5:16).

Evidence From Mystical Religious Experiences

For many years, I have researched the psychology of religious experience and taught it in course format several times. People in my classes generally fall into the same two categories as the public at large, i.e., those who accept the ongoing revelation of God through mystical experiences and those who intellectually cannot grasp it. I tell them that mystical religious experiences have been reported by saints, mystics, and ordinary people throughout all ages and cultures. Mysticism is the direct experience of God or as the great Anglican mystic Evelyn Underhill put it: "the simple yet utterly inexpressible union of the soul with its God." Those who have had mystical religious experiences offer insights into God's powerful and engulfing love.

A wide variety of Christian denominations from Roman Catholics to Quakers acknowledge that valid mystical experiences of God continue to occur. Only a few denominations maintain that religious revelation was "sealed" when the *New Testament* was completed. For those who consider the *Bible* the only trusted authority for God, the *Bible* verses supporting Universal Restoration can certainly stand on their own, without any additional validation from post-Biblical sources. However, if your skepticism about the use of non-Biblical religious experience is based on a fear that it may not come from God, it helps to recall the words of Jesus. When Jesus was accused of being Satanic (Mk 3:22-26), he explained that evil cannot rise up against evil. Jesus also told us how to distinguish false prophets: **"You will know them by their fruits"** (Matt 7:16). The fruits of the Holy Spirit are wholly good (Gal 5:22-23). For me, it is easy to see evidence of the ongoing presence of God in our lives revealed continuously to mystics throughout the 2,000 years since the *Bible* was written.

Unfortunately, proponents of the occult like to masquerade as mystics, but there is a simple difference. The occult seeks to enhance the supernormal powers of the individual, often to the disadvantage of another person. The occult is all about "me, me, me!" Mystical religious experiences are always about God, and "Nothing evil comes from God" (Jas 1:13-17).

Over the past few years, academic researchers have attempted to study mysticism from a sociological, psychological, and physiological viewpoint in order to gain a more objective perspective on this phenomenon. The National Opinion Research Institute at the University of Chicago and the Religious Research Centre at Oxford University have found through national surveys that about 40% of us have been blessed with a mystical experience. This mystical chain of love that goes on forever serves to continually validate the *Bible*'s message of God's love.

The Universalist theologian John Hick bases his Universalism in part on his own mystical experiences of God, and I do too. God has never stopped communicating with us. Mystical experiences, religious visions, death-bed visions, post-death visions, and modern day near-death experiences are all testimony to the fact that God's loving presence is more powerful than we can imagine. They also serve as ongoing validation of the *Bible*'s message that God is always present (Eph 4:6) and that God's love for us is unconditional (Lam 3:22).

Universalism Resonates

The *Golden Thread* of Universalism begins with God's good creation, continues through the Hebrew prophets, and culminates with Jesus' teachings. Jesus' ministry brings us the Word and shows us the Way so that we can recognize the Kingdom of God within us (Lk 17:20-21). In the preceding chapters we have been told that God's love is universal and after a **"time of trial"** (Matt 6:13) for some there will be salvation for *all* (I Tim 4:10). Universalism does not require a change of denomination; it takes a change of heart.

This book is an answer for all who have wondered about the fate of their non-Christian loved ones. For me, the quest began in childhood with my question to my Universalist Great Aunt Alice about where the *Bible* said *all* people go to Heaven. When we think of how to explain Christian Universalism to a child, it is easy. Start with the fact that God is the parent of *all* and the best parent ever. Jesus teaches us this at the beginning of the Lord's Prayer: **"Our Father"** (Matt 6:9). Next, tell the story of the "Lost Sheep" (Matt 18:10-14). Explain that God is the Good Shepherd who loves *all* of us and will never give up until *all* of us are safely home. See? You knew about Universalism all along, and you did not know it!

The *Bible* you have known since childhood contains all the evidence necessary for Universalism. In this book, I have assembled the verses that Universalists throughout the ages have used to support their view. Some of the Universalist verses used are cited by virtually all Universalist sources, while others have been cited by fewer. The complete listings of all the verses that I have located are in the Appendices of this book. The more I became engrossed in my study of the Universalist message, the more the *Bible* in general and the *New Testament* in particular began to resonate with the God of hope, joy, and love. God lives in us and we live in God (Eph 4:6). In the end, God will be "all in all" (I Cor 15:28).

Epilogue

The following four summaries which are in Responsive Reading format assure us that God saves us, that we are *all* the children of God, and that though we are *all* accountable to God, in the end *all* will be united with God.

God is the one who saves us!

God is light.
God is light and in him there is no darkness at all (I Jn 1:5). Every generous act of giving, with every perfect gift, is from above, coming down from the Father of lights (Jas 1:17)….he who is the blessed and only Sovereign, the King of kings and Lord of lords. It is he alone who has immortality and dwells in unapproachable light…(I Tim 6:15-16).

God is Spirit.
God is spirit, and those who worship him must worship in spirit and truth (Jn 4:24). No one has ever seen God; if we love one another, God lives in us, and his love is perfected in us. By this we know that we abide in him and he in us, because he has given us his Spirit (I Jn 4:12-13).

God is our salvation.
Surely God is my salvation; I will trust, and not be afraid, for the Lord God is my strength and my might; he has become my salvation (Is 12:2).

God is in all.
For "In him we live and move and have our being" (Acts 17:28). For from him and through him and to him are all things (Rom 11:36). One God and Father of all, who is above all and through all and in all (Eph 4:6).

God is love.
Beloved, let us love one another, because love is from God; everyone who loves is born of God and knows God. Whoever does not love does not know God, for God is love (I Jn 4:7-8).

God's love is unconditional.
He makes his sun rise on the evil and on the good, and sends rain on the righteous and on the unrighteous (Matt 5:45).

God's kingdom cannot be seen with our eyes.
God's Kingdom is coming, but not in a way that you will be able to see it with your eyes. People will not say, "Look, here it is!" or "There it is!" because, the kingdom of God is within you (Lk 17:20-21, NCV). No eye has seen, nor ear heard, nor the human heart conceived, what God has prepared for those who love him (I Cor 2:9).

Jesus says his Father and our Father are the same.
Our Father in heaven (Matt 6:9). **You have one Father—the one in Heaven** (Matt 23:9). **I am ascending to my Father and your Father, to my God and your God** (Jn 20:17).

Whose child are you?

Whose child are you?
When we cry, "**Abba! Father!**" it is that very Spirit bearing witness with our spirit that we are the children of God (Rom 8:16).

Whose child are you?
We are the children of Wisdom (Sophia) who tells us, "Now, my children, listen to me: happy are those who keep my ways" (Prov 8:32).

Whose child are you?
We are all the children of the light and the children of the day; we are not of the night or of darkness (I Thes 5:5).

Whose child are you?
See what love the Father has given us, that we should be called the Children of God (I Jn: 3:1).

Whose child are you?
For the one who sacrifices and those who are sanctified all have one Father. For this reason, Jesus is not ashamed to call them brothers and sisters (Heb 2:11).

Whose child are you?
Jesus says, **"You have one Father—the one in heaven"** (Matt 23:9) and **"You have One instructor, the Messiah"** (Matt 23:10).

Whose child are you?
All who are led by the Spirit of God are the Children of God (Rom 8:14).

Come Judgment Day!

Will we be held accountable?
Each of us will be accountable to God (Rom 14:12).

How will we be judged?
For with the judgment you make you will be judged (Matt 7:2).

Will words alone save us?
Not everyone who says to me, "Lord, Lord" will enter the kingdom of heaven, but only the one who does the will of my Father in heaven (Matt 7:21).

Will our good words and deeds save us?
You reap whatever you sow (Gal 6:7).

Will God save those who are not Christians?
God shows no partiality, but in every nation anyone who fears him and does what is right is acceptable to him (Acts 10:34-35).

Will justice ever reign?
Anyone who does wrong will be punished for that wrong, and the Lord treats everyone the same (Col 3:25, NCV).

How long will the wicked suffer?
Until each pays, "**his entire debt**" (Matt 18:34).

Who shall See God?

Who shall be saved?
All flesh shall see the salvation of God (Lk 3:6).

Who does God want to be saved?
God "desires everyone to be saved and to come to the knowledge of the truth. For there is one God; there is also one mediator between God and humankind, Christ Jesus, himself human, who gave himself a ransom for all" (I Tim 2:4-6).

Who shall worship God?
The Lord says, "All flesh shall come to worship before me" (Is 66:23).

Who shall sit at the table of the Lord?
On this mountain the Lord of hosts will make for all peoples a feast (Is 25:6).

Even those who have gone astray?
It is not the will of your Father in heaven that one of these little ones shall be lost (Matt 18:14).

Who shall be taught by God?
They shall all be taught by God (Jn 6:45).

Who does God forgive?
This is the Covenant that I will make with them after those days, says the Lord: I will put my laws in their hearts, and I will write them on their minds," he also adds, "I will remember their sins and their lawless deeds no more" (Heb 10:16-17).

When will the restoration come?
He has made known to us the mystery of his will, according to his good pleasure set forth in Christ, as a plan for the fullness of time, to gather up all things in him, things in Heaven and things on earth (Eph 1:9-10).

What do we strive for?
For to this end do we toil and struggle, because we have our hope set on the living God, who is Savior of all people, especially those who believe (I Tim 4:10).

Who shall see God?
The grace of God has appeared, bringing salvation to all (Titus 2:11).

Appendices

APPENDIX A

New Testament Verses Supporting Salvation by Works

✦

(551 verses - 389 in Jesus' words)

<u>Matthew</u> All of Chapters 5,6, &7 "Sermon on the Mount" (Esp. 5:16;6:14; 6:20-21;7:1-2,21) ;9:13; 12:33-37; 13:1-30, 36-43,47-50; 15:10-20; 16:27; 18:7-9, 21-35; 19:16-22; 21:28-31; 22:8-14, 37-40; 24:45-51; 25:31-46
<u>Mark</u> 4:1-20, 22-24; 9:43-48; 10:17-22; 11:25; 12:29-34, 38-44
<u>Luke</u> 6:27-49; 7:47; 8:4-15;10:25-37; 11:4,34-36; 12:2-5,16-21,33-34,48,57-59; 13:6-9; 14:12-14; 16:19-31; 18:9-14,18-23; 19:1-10; 21:1-4; 22:27
<u>John</u> 5:28-29
<u>Acts</u> 10:34-35; 17:31
<u>Romans</u> 2:1-16,27-29; 3:3-4; 11:21-22; 12:9-21; 13:8-10,12; 14:10-12
<u>I Corinthians</u> 4:4-5; 7:19
<u>II Corinthians</u> 5:10; 9:6-12; 11:15
<u>Galatians</u> 5:14; 6:7-10
<u>Ephesians</u> 6:1-9
<u>Colossians</u> 3:25
<u>I Timothy</u> 5:8
<u>Hebrews</u> 13:1-6, 16
<u>James</u> 1:12,22-25,27; 2:8-26; 3:1,13; 4:8-12; 5:1-15,19-20
<u>I Peter</u> 1:17; 3:8-12; 4:5, 8, 17-19
<u>II Peter</u> 2:4-9, 3:8-13
<u>I John</u> 2:9-11, 17; 3:7-8; 4:20-21
<u>III John</u> 1:11
<u>Revelation</u> 20:11-15; 21:6-8

APPENDIX B

New Testament Verses Supporting Universal Salvation

◆

(231 verses + Hell not Permanent 42 verses = 273 verses)

Matthew 5:43-45; 11:28-30; 18:12-14; 19:26; 20:1-15
Mark 10:27
Luke 2:10, 29-32; 3:4-6; 6:35-36; 15:3-6,8-9,11-32; 18:27; 19:10; 20:38, 23:34
John 1:9, 29; 3:17; 4:42; 5:22; 6:37-39, 45; 8:15 (Note: 5:22 & 8:15 read together); 10:16; 12:32; 17:2; 20:17
Acts 3:20-21, 25-26; 13:47; 24:15
Romans 5:6-8,12-18; 6:14, 23; 8:19-23, 38-39; 11:25-36; 14:7-8, 11
I Corinthians 15:22-28, 42-55
II Corinthians 3:18; 5:14, 18-19
Galatians 3:8
Ephesians 1:9-10, 20-23; 2:7; 4:6,13
Philippians 2:9-11; 3:21
Colossians 1:19-20
I Timothy 2:1-6; 4:10
Titus 2:11; 3:4-7
Hebrews 2:9, 14-15; 8:6-12; 10:10, 15-17
James 1:17
II Peter 3:9
I John 2:1-2; 3:19-20; 4: 7-11, 14, 16, 19
Revelation 5:13, 15:4, 21:1-5; 22:2,17

Sub-Category of Universal Salvation, i.e., Hell Not Permanent (42 verses)

Matthew 5:25-26; 18:23-35
Mark 9:49
Luke 3:16; 12:47-49, 57-59
I Corinthians 3:14-15; 10:13; 11:32
Ephesians 4:9-10
Hebrews 12:5-11, 29
I Peter 3:18-20; 4:6
Revelation 1:18

APPENDIX C

Old Testament (Hebrew Bible) Verses Supporting Universal Salvation

✦

(81 verses + Hell Not Permanent 29 verses = 110 verses)

Genesis 1:31; 22:18
II Samuel 14:14
Psalms 22:27; 25:8; 37:23-24; 62:1; 65:2; 86:9; 89:2, 14; 100:5; 103:1-4; 107:1; 136:1; 139:8; 145:8-10, 14, 21
Ecclesiastes 12:7
Isaiah 2:2, 4; 11:6-9; 12:1-2; 25:6-8; 40:3-5, 10-11; 43:25; 45:21-25; 49:6, 14-15; 52:10; 56:7; 61:1-2; 66:18, 23
Jeremiah 31:31-34
Lamentations 3:22
Ezekiel 16: 46-49, 53-56, 59-63
Daniel 7:13-14
Hosea 11:9
Joel 2:28-29
Malachi 1:11; 2:10

Sub-Category of Universal Salvation, i.e., Hell Not Permanent (29 verses)

Psalms 30:5; 89:30-33; 99:8; 103:8-9
Isaiah 4:4; 24:21-23; 54:8; 57:16

Lamentations 3:31-33
Ezekiel 36:25-27
Hosea 13:14; 14:4
Micah 7:18-20
Zephaniah 3:8-9
Malachi 3:2-3

APPENDIX D

Funeral Service Stressing Universal Salvation

God is light and in him there is no darkness at all (I Jn 1:5).

God is the one who saves me; I will trust him and not be afraid. The Lord, the Lord gives me strength and makes me sing. He has saved me (Is 12:2, NCV).

Master, now you are dismissing your servant in peace, according to your word; for my eyes have seen your salvation which you have prepared in the presence of all peoples (Lk 2:29-31).

All flesh shall see the salvation of God (Lk 3:6).

The Lord All-Powerful will prepare a feast on this mountain for all people. It will be a feast with all the best food and wine, the finest meat and wine. On this mountain God will destroy the veil that covers all nations, the veil that stretches over all peoples; he will destroy death forever. The Lord God will wipe away every tear from every face. He will take away the shame of his people from the earth. The Lord has spoken (Is 25:6-9, NCV).

And the Holy Spirit also testifies to us, for after saying, "This is the covenant that I will make with them after those days, says the Lord: I will put my laws in their hearts and I will write them on their minds." He also adds, "I will remember their sins and their lawless deeds no more" (Heb 10:15-17).

Jesus assures us of an afterlife.
Now he is God not of the dead, but of the living; for to him all of them are alive (Lk 20:38).

Jesus says that God is our Father too.
I am ascending to my Father and your Father, to my God and your God (Jn 20:17).

Jesus promises that all will be with him in Paradise.
And I, when I am lifted up from the earth, will draw all people to myself (Jn 12:32).

This is right and is acceptable in the sight of God our Savior, who desires everyone to be saved and to come to the knowledge of the truth. For there is one God; there is also one mediator between God and humankind, Christ Jesus, himself human who gave himself a ransom for all (I Tim 2:3-6).

When all things are subjected to him, then the Son himself will also be subjected to the one who put all things in subjection under him, so that God may be all in all (I Cor 15:28).

(Insert Eulogy)

Eventually all will be united with God.
For to this end we toil and struggle, because we have our hope set on the living God, who is the Savior of all people, especially of those who believe (I Tim 4:10).

For the grace of God has appeared bringing salvation to all (Titus 2:11).

For a child or mystic add:
Jesus said, **Let the little children come to me; do not stop them; for it is to such as these that the kingdom of God belongs. Truly I tell you, whoever, does not receive the kingdom of God as a little child will never enter it** (Mk 10:14-15).

Let us pray:
Our Father in heaven,
Hallowed be your name.
Your kingdom come.
Your will be done,
On earth as it is in heaven.
Give us this day our daily bread.
And forgive us our debts
As we also have forgiven our debtors.
And do not bring us to the time of trial,
But rescue us from the evil one (Matt 6:9-13).

For it is written, "What no eye has seen, nor ear heard, nor the human heart conceived, what God has prepared for those who love him" (1 Cor 2:9).

Appendix E

Funeral Service for a Beloved Pet

And God said, "Let the earth bring forth living creatures of every kind: cattle and creeping things and wild animals of the earth of every kind." And it was so. God made the wild animals of the earth of every kind, and the cattle of every kind, and everything that creeps upon the ground of every kind. And God saw that it was good (Gen 1:24-25).

Your righteousness is like the mighty mountains, your judgments are like the great deep; you save humans and animals alike, O Lord (Ps 36:6).

Ask the animals, and they will teach you; the birds of the air, and they will tell you; ask the plants of the earth, and they will teach you; and the fish of the sea will declare to you. Who among all these does not know that the hand of the Lord has done this? In his hand is the life of every living thing (Job 12:7-10).

For the fate of humans and the fate of animals is the same; as one dies, so dies the other. They all have the same breath, and humans have no advantage over the animals (Eccl 3:19).

Just as it was written:
"The ox knows its owner and the donkey its master's crib" (Is 1:3).
So the animals were present at the Birth of Jesus.

Paul tells us in his letters:
He has made known to us the mystery of his will, according to his good pleasure that he set forth in Christ, as a plan for the fullness of time, to gather up all things in him, things in heaven and things on earth (Eph 1:8-10).

When all things are subjected to him then the Son himself will also be subjected to the one who put all things in subjection under him, so that God may be all in all (I Cor 15:28).

The gospel that you heard has been proclaimed by every creature under heaven (Col 1:23).

Jesus expressed God's love for the animals.
Are not five sparrows sold for two pennies? Yet not one of them is forgotten in God's sight (Lk 12:6).

All life celebrates the glory of God!
Then I heard every creature in heaven and on earth and under the earth and in the sea, and all that is in them singing, "To the one seated on the throne and to the Lamb be blessing and honor and glory and might forever and ever" (Rev 5:13).

(Insert Eulogy)

Just as it was at the creation, so shall it be in the end time of the New Heaven and the New Earth. Surely we shall all be together in the Peaceful Kingdom of God.
Then wolves will live in peace with lambs, and leopards will lie down to rest with the goats. Calves, lions, and young bulls will eat together, and a little child will lead them. Cows and bears will eat together in peace. Their young will lie down and rest together. Lions will eat hay as oxen do. A baby will be able to play near a cobra's hole, and a child will be able to put his hand into the nest of a poisonous snake. They will not hurt or destroy each other on all my holy mountain, because the earth will be full of the knowledge of the LORD, as the sea is full of water (Is 11:6-9, NCV).

APPENDIX F

Funeral Service for a Non-Christian in a Christian Family

(*These Bible verses are appropriate for use in a service for an individual who is unaffiliated with any church or religion.*)

God is light and in him there is no darkness at all (I Jn 1:5).

For from the rising of the sun to its setting my name is great among the nations, and in every place incense is offered to my name, and a pure offering, for my name is great among the nations, says the Lord of hosts (Mal 1:11).

For everything there is a season and a time for every matter under heaven: a time to be born, and a time to die; a time to plant, and a time to pluck up what is planted; a time to kill, and a time to heal; a time to break down, and a time to build up; a time to weep, and a time to laugh; a time to mourn, and a time to dance; a time to throw away stones, and a time to gather stones together; a time to embrace, and a time to refrain from embracing; a time to seek, and a time to lose; a time to keep, and a time to throw away; a time to tear, and a time to sew; a time to keep silence, and a time to speak; a time to love, and a time to hate; a time for war, and a time for peace (Eccl 3:1-8).

God shows no partiality, but in every nation anyone who fears him and does what is right is acceptable to him (Acts 10:34).

In Matthew, God (the Good Shepherd) seeks and saves the lost sheep; the sheep does not return to the flock of its own accord. The parable ends, **"So it is not the will of your Father in Heaven that one of these little ones should be lost"** (Matt 18:14).

In the story of the Prodigal Son (Lk 15:11-24), the returning son does not ask to be a member of the family but for a job as his father's servant. He tells his Father, *"Father, I have sinned against heaven and before you; I am no longer worthy to be called you son; treat me like one of your hired hands"* (Lk 15:19). It is God (the father) who takes him back into the family. The father is the character with the active role. People often have difficulty with this story because they wrongly identify with the good son and not with the father. Considering how much human parents love their children, the story puts some perspective on how much God, who is all good, loves each of us.

For a child, add the following:
Jesus said to them, **"Let the little children come to me; do not stop them; for it is to such as these that the kingdom of God belongs. Truly I tell you, whoever does not receive the kingdom of God as a little child will never enter it"** (Mk 10:14-15).

(Insert Eulogy)

The Lord All-Powerful will prepare a feast on this mountain for all people. It will be a feast with all the best food and wine, the finest meat and wine. On this mountain God will destroy the veil that covers all nations, the veil that stretches over all peoples; he will destroy death forever. The Lord God will wipe away every tear from every face. He will take away the shame of his people from the earth. The Lord has spoken (Is 25:6-9, NCV).

The Lord is gracious and merciful, slow to anger and abounding in steadfast love. The Lord is good to all, and his compassion is over all that he has made. The Lord upholds all who are falling, and raises up all who are bowed down (Ps 145:8-9,14).

And all flesh shall see the salvation of God (Lk 3:6).

May the Lord bless you and keep you. May the Lord show you his kindness and have mercy on you. May the Lord watch over you and give you peace (Num 6:24-26, NCV).

APPENDIX G

Christian Universalism "Endorsed" by Jesus Seminar

(**Note**: This article was first published in the *Universalist Herald*, Sept./Oct. 2004, Vol. 155,(5).)

Validating the doctrine of Christian Universalism was not one of the Jesus Seminar's stated objectives. Nevertheless, in their efforts to determine the genuine words and deeds of the historical Jesus, the Seminar has confirmed that Jesus' message of Universal Salvation is authentic to him. Christian Universalism is the belief that God is too good to condemn anyone to eternal hell and that *all* people will be eventually reconciled with God. It is a position strongly supported in *Bible* and advocated by Christians from the 1st Century to the present. Unfortunately, it is a message often overlooked or ignored in many Christian pulpits, despite its particular relevance for our modern, pluralistic world.

As many Christians already know, the Jesus Seminar undertook a unique experiment in tapping the knowledge of over 200 academicians and theologians from various backgrounds to separate the authentic words and deeds of the historical Jesus from later editing. As a religious writer, I am extremely grateful for the time and expertise devoted to this project. As a social scientist, I have particular respect for their attempts to find an objective method for their research. Unfortunately, I believe that the color-coding method chosen has fostered some unfortunate distortions and misunderstandings of their conclusions.

Briefly, the Jesus Seminar scholars coded red the words they deemed unique to Jesus; those words of Jesus with less consensus were colored pink. I had read through their first major work, *The Five Gospels*, for a third time before it dawned on me that the red and pink words did not represent words spoken by Jesus but those utterances that were *absolutely new* and original to him—the stuff that separated the Messiah from the earlier prophets. When I talk about this in Sunday school, I challenge people in an exercise to help them understand how rare "red" words occur in life. I ask them to think about the thoughts they express which are entirely fresh—not borrowed from their parents, relatives, teachers, preachers, books, or media. Once they concentrate on this, they realize how little is truly "unique!"

Those words deemed "in the spirit" of Jesus or "similar" to Jesus were coded gray. Those that did not represent Jesus' unique message were coded black. The black words fall into three categories: 1) Statements in which Jesus quotes the *Hebrew Bible*, 2) Statements from common lore, and 3) Propaganda added by the early churches/writers. Unfortunately, the words colored gray or black are often interpreted by many to mean that "Jesus never said that" when, in fact, those words may have been uttered by Jesus but were not considered by the Jesus Seminar scholars to be original to him. Like virtually every preacher, prophet, sage, and saint who has ever lived, Jesus surely quoted from Scripture; we can also be certain that he referred to common lore (i.e., common sense, the type of wisdom found in *Proverbs*), as well as statements compatible with wisdom from other religions in the ancient world. The question then becomes: Are the quotes from the *Bible* and common lore consistent with the authentic teachings of Jesus? In my opinion, the Jesus Seminar needed several more colors!

Christian Universalism, also known as Universal Restoration or Universal Salvation, is the idea expressed in the *Bible* that God's love is so great that, after rehabilitation/purification in Hell for those who don't measure up, *all* will be saved. There are a substantial number of *Bible* verses cited by Universalist theologians from ancient times to the present to make the case for Christian Universalism, especially when the verses supporting Salvation by Good Works are included to make the case for Universal Restoration.

Except for the *Bible* itself, the first theologian to write about Universalism was Clement of Alexandria (150-215 CE). His pupil, Origen (185-254 CE), further developed the understanding of Universalism and is considered the major ancient authority on the subject. After Universalism was declared a heresy by the Roman Catholic Church in the Sixth Century, it continued to be advocated by some theologians in the East and mystics in the West. With the Reformation, there was a re-birth of Universalist thought, and for a time the Universalist Church of America was the sixth largest denomination in the United States. Its demise is often attributed to its success, as other churches began to de-emphasize predestination and fire and brimstone in favor of the more loving message of God's love for *all*. The Universalist church merged with the Unitarian church in 1961, and the movement has become an interfaith church in which Universalist Christians have become an ever decreasing minority. Most people today who endorse Universalist theology can be found in virtually all Christian denominations; Universalism requires a change of heart but not necessarily a change of denomination. Examples of prominent Universalists include William Barclay (Presbyterian), Jan Bonda (Dutch Reformed), Philip Gulley and James Mulholland (Quakers), Tom Harpur (Anglican), John Hick (United Reformed), Randy Klassen (Mennonite), Dennis, Sheila, and Matthew Linn (Roman Catholics), John A. T. Robinson (Anglican), Thomas Talbott (Independent), and Hans von Balthasar (Roman Catholic).

Now let us look at how various theological positions found in the Gospels fared with the Jesus Seminar. The verses are somewhat vexing to analyze, as the scholars often assign three different colors to a single verse! Significantly, all of the verses relating to the "Jesus Saves" theology were rejected as original to Jesus. John Calvin's Predestination fared only slightly better with only two verses seen as original to Jesus (Matt 6:10, 10:29). Some classic sayings of Jesus on Good Works were deemed authentic, although two of the mainstay examples of good works were rejected, i.e., The Judgment of the Nations (also known as The Parable of the Sheep and the Goats) (Matt 25:31-46) and The Parable of the Rich Man and Lazarus (Luke 16:19-31). The former was seen as early church propaganda, and the latter thought suspect, as it was similar to stories from other religions in the ancient world. Verses relating to good works that were voted authentic include: Parable of the Good Samaritan (Luke 10:30-35), Jesus on forgiveness (Matt 6:12), and the Parable of the Sower (Mk 4:3-8; Matt 13:3-8; Lk 8:5-8).

By far, passages advocating Universal Salvation received endorsement from the Jesus Seminar as most authentic to Jesus. While they rejected some of the "zingers" (e.g., Jn 12:32), virtually all Jesus' classic parables interpreted as Universalist were judged by the Jesus Seminar to be genuine to him, including: The Parable of the Lost Sheep (Matt 18:12-13; Lk 15:4-6), The Workers in the Vineyard (Matt 20:1-15), The Parable of the Lost Coin (Lk 15:8-9), and the Parable of the Prodigal Son (Lk 15:11-32). Also, the verses relating to the fact that Hell is not permanent and used only for rehabilitation/purification were determined authentic by the Jesus Seminar. They are: Settle with Your Opponent (Matt 5:25-26; Lk 12:58-59) and the Parable of the Wicked Servant (Matt 18:23-34). Finally, although it was mutilated in part by the Jesus Seminar scholars, Jesus' teaching to be like God and love our enemies as God is good to the just and the unjust (Matt 5:44-46) was voted genuine to Jesus.

In spite of the controversy surrounding the minimalist approach to the Gospels used by the Jesus Seminar, Christian Universalists can take some satisfaction that the theology that emerges is an unwitting endorsement of the teachings of Jesus that have been used by Universalist theologians from the Second Century forward as expressing God's Universal Love for *all* people and, after a "time of trial" for some (Matt 6:13), the promise of Salvation for *all* people.

APPENDIX H

Magic, Deeds, and Universalism

(**Note**: This article was first published in the *Universalist Herald*, July/Aug. 2005, Vol. 156,(4).)

When I was a freshman at Baylor University, I took a required religion class from Prof. Kyle Yates. Professor Yates was one of the scholars who worked on the *Revised Standard Version of the Old Testament* (a.k.a. the *Hebrew Bible*). When we got to the Persian period of Hebrew history, he began to talk about Zoroaster, the prophet of the Magi. Inspired by his lectures, I went to the library and read the Hymns of Zoroaster and thought to myself, "Wow! God talked to someone who wasn't Jewish!" This started my life-long quest for the generic God in the world's religions.

For many years, I've been active in interfaith work, and my friends and colleagues here in Houston form a tapestry of the world's religions. I have learned from them. Now that I'm retired, I'm a little old man who lives on the fourth floor of the Rice University Library, still steeped in the world's religions.

Today, I will be your guide to the Afterlife. You may have been hoping for Beatrice and Dante, but the editor wasn't quite able to conjure them up. I'm going to give you a three-layer view of how people—both ancient and modern—have viewed Afterlife. This is what we in psychology call a "developmental" view of religion because it reflects the way both individuals and societies normally mature.

The most rudimentary level of religious development is *Magic*, which includes bribery or other manipulation of God or the gods in order to guarantee a positive outcome for your Afterlife. In the middle layer, Afterlife is dependent on your *Deeds* during your life on Earth, and the history of religious art illustrates the development of this idea across time and cultures. Interestingly, Magic has often been practiced in conjunction with Good Deeds. The top layer of development is *Universalism*, the concept that God is too good to condemn anyone to Eternal Hell, and that all humans will go to Heaven, either immediately or eventually.

One important thing to know about the study of comparative religion is that it is a wide-open field with many scholars from various disciplines participating, such as Joseph Campbell (literature), Mircea Eliade (history), Paul Brunton (philosophy), Karl Jung (psychiatry), and Sir James Frazier (anthropology). We are going to touch on the Afterlife from the perspectives of religion, history, psychology, sociology, and art.

Most people in the world, regardless of their religion, believe that judgment for the Afterlife is determined by one's deeds in this life. Simply stated, if your good deeds outweigh your bad deeds, you go to Heaven. But if your bad deeds outweigh your good deeds, you go to Hell. This is the story of humanity. My point is that human beings across time and culture share one story, although I must tell you that in the East, after an intermediate stage of Heaven or Hell, you have a "sequel"—called "reincarnation." In other words, in the East, your deeds affect not only your intermediate destination of Heaven or Hell, but also determine the condition of your next life.

The oldest judgment scene we have in art is a depiction of the *Egyptian Book of the Dead* which has been seen in tomb art as early as about 3,000 BCE. After the deceased goes into the darkness (which is the body of Nut), he or she comes forth into the light, into the Great Hall of Truth. Osiris is the King of the Afterlife, and Isis is his queen. For over 3,500 years, Osiris was known as the "Resurrection and the Life." Your deeds in life were judged by weighing your heart against a feather, and woe to those whose heart is heavy with sin!

Next we have judgment in Zoroastrianism, the religion of the Magi. Here, three angels preside over judgment—Mithra, Sarosha, and Rashnu. Rashnu holds the scales, Sarosha is the judge, and Mithra listens to appeals. Your good deeds are weighed against your bad deeds, and then you pass over a bridge. If your good deeds are heavier, the bridge is wide open to you, and you pass over easily. If your evil deeds outweigh your good ones, the bridge becomes narrow, and you fall into Hell. This razor-sharp bridge imagery lives on in Shiite Islam.

In the *Hebrew Bible*, in the Book of Daniel (12:1-3), it is the Archangel Michael who presides over the resurrection. Judaism for the most part forbids artwork, but in Christianity, Michael takes his place right below Jesus in the judgment of the dead. It is Michael who holds the scales in which your deeds are weighed. This same scene is repeated in Islam, except that the Archangel holding the scales is Gabriel.

Next we move from West to East. Most Westerners think that reincarnation is instantaneous, but this is not generally so. For the overwhelming majority of Hindus and Buddhists, there is an intermediate state between death and re-birth.

This intermediate state is presided over by Yama or Yamaraj. In Hindu religion, Yama was the first king and king of the dead. His assistants weigh your good deeds and, depending on the outcome, you go to Heaven or Hell for three generations. In Buddhism, as in its parent religion, Yama judges the dead. Yama is known as "Yama" in Tibet, Nepal, Southeast Asia and Western China. In Eastern China, Korea, and Japan, his name changes, but he is always the same fair judge of the dead. Where he is the king of Heaven in Hinduism, he presides over Hell in Buddhism. In the *Tibetan Book of the Dead*, a twelfth-century Buddhist work, the intermediate state lasts for 49 days before you are re-born.

Now let's step back to analyze the way Magic is used to influence Afterlife. Obviously, we are aware of cultures in both the Eastern and Western hemispheres that have used human or animal sacrifice to bribe God or the gods to do or *not* do something the petitioner asks. However, this practice has been abandoned by the world's major religions. On the other hand, belief in magical powers is still very much a part of our modern culture when it comes to "stacking the deck" in favor of a Heavenly Afterlife!

In most religions, there is a tension between the moral justice of judgment according to deeds and magic to insure a positive verdict. The keys to effective magic are that, 1) You have to be "in the club," and 2) You or your priest must know the "secret words."

In ancient Egypt, the scales of judgment are older than the pyramids, but they co-exist with the magic text of the *Egyptian Book of the Dead* that enables the deceased to overcome past sins. Countering this are not only the scales, but the instruction for Merikare (2200 BCE) which reinforces the idea of judgment according to deeds.

Additionally, there is the story of Si-Osiris (son of Osiris) and his father, Setne Khaemwise (fourth son of Ramesses II). Si-Osiris is a seer. He and his father watch a funeral procession in which a rich man was being carried with his elaborate belongings to a princely tomb. Shortly after this, they observed the funeral of a poor man wrapped only in a cloth who was being taken for burial in the desert sand. The Egyptian prince remarks to his son that he hopes for a good funeral in preparation for a glorious Afterlife, but his seer son remarks that all things are not as they appear to be. He puts his father into a trance, and the two are transported to the land of the dead where the evil rich man is suffering a hellish fate and the righteous poor man is being comforted by Osiris, Isis, and the Egyptian gods, and is living afterlife in regal splendor.

This shows the development of morality and justice in the Egyptian religion, and some Christian scholars think this is the origin of the story of the rich man and Lazarus in the Gospel of Luke (Lk 16:19-31). The main point here is to underscore the great antiquity of the belief that salvation is by works.

In ancient Greece, the Afterlife in very early times was seen as a gloomy place where everyone dwelled. But by the time of Plato, the idea of judgment according to deeds had developed. In Plato's *Republic*, the story is told about Er, the world's oldest recorded near-death experiencer, who revives on his funeral pyre and tells of a judgment at death by three judges. The good ascend to Paradise, and the evil descend to Hell. Plato mentions the possibility of reincarnation, and Pythagoras was an advocate of reincarnation. In the mysteries that were popular in the later Greek and Roman periods, people were given a chance for an "up-grade" in the Afterlife via the magical rites of the mysteries of Orpheus, Dionysus, Demeter and Persephone, Mithra, Isis and Osiris, etc. According to the mysteries of Orpheus, one of the things one was to say was, "I am a child of Earth and the starry Heaven, but Heaven is my home." Here again, you have to be in the club, and you have to know the secret words!

In ancient Judaism, the sins of the Jewish people were magically put into a goat (scapegoat) on the Day of Atonement. As before, you have to be "in the club" and you (or the priest) must know the secret words (Lev. 16:21-22). Modern Jews no longer do this, knowing that God hears our prayers.

Judaism in its early years presented a shadowy Afterlife called Sheol which was very similar to the Hades of early Greece. Jewish writing from 400-100 BCE found in the Catholic, Orthodox, Eastern Orthodox, and Coptic Christian *Bibles* (which Protestants refer to as the *Apocrypha*) have references to prayers for the dead so that their sins may be blotted out in the Afterlife (II Maccabees 12:44-45). The Apocryphal books also abound with angels who are named (e.g. Raphael in the Book of Tobit). The Jewish Pseudepigrapha (200 BCE-70 CE) have Heaven and Hell (especially Enoch I, II, and III). These books of Enoch are not in the *Hebrew Bible*, and only 1st Enoch made it into the Coptic Christian *Bible*. These books were, however, used by the Essenes and figure into Judaism prior to the destruction of the Temple in 70 CE. The Rule of Community (also known as the Manual of Discipline) and the War of the Sons of Light and the Sons of Darkness in the *Dead Sea Scrolls* of the Essenes are especially rich in imagery of Heaven and Hell. After 70 CE, Rabbinic Judaism developed, and the resulting *Hebrew Bible* has references to Sheol, the Messianic Time, and the Last Judgment in the Book of Daniel.

In Christianity, this magic level is practiced by those who say that "belief in Jesus" assures an exclusive ticket to Heaven. You have to be "in the club" (that is, be a Christian), and you have to know the secret words, which for Fundamentalist Christianity are found in John 3:16 or John 14:6. While Liberal Christians and many moderate Christians see Jesus as the "suffering servant" of Isaiah who died bringing us the Word, Fundamentalist Christians delight in being "saved." That belief alone will save you is an idea as old as the followers of the Hindu god Lord Krishna. Its positive side is the devotional path in which the followers identify with and emulate the god. In Christianity, we see this positive emulation in those kind and loving souls who model their lives on Jesus. One is reminded of the words of the beautiful old Gospel hymn, "In the Garden": "He walks with me, and He talks with me, and He tells me I am His own." In Hinduism, the devotional path is expressed in the prayer, "Krishna, Krishna, Hare, Hare," in other words, "Krishna, Krishna, Redeemer, Redeemer."

Magic in Hinduism is best illustrated by the idea that if you die with the name of Vishnu or one of his incarnations (such as Rama or Krishna) on your lips, all of your sins are taken away and you go straight to Nirvana (heaven). There are times when we all need a little magic. Reportedly, the last words of Gandhi were, "Rama, Rama."

In Buddhism, magic is represented in the *Tibetan Book of the Dead*. Being "in the club" (that is, being Buddhist) and having your relative or a monk read the secret words of the *Book of the Dead* by your corpse will enable you to become aware in the Afterlife and choose the things which will assure you a good re-birth. Also in Pure Land Buddhism, by invoking the name of the Buddha at death, you will be transported to a Pure Land of Bliss in the West by Amitabha (the Buddha of Infinite Light), who is also known as O-Mi-To (China) and Amida (Japan). There you can continue the process of liberation under blissful conditions. Another Bodhisattva (savior) is Ti-tsang, and anyone who chants his name will have his/her sins wiped away.

Having looked at the developmental level below judgment by deeds, let us look at the level above it—Universalism. The concept of Universalism as an idea is as old as Zoroaster. Around 1600-1200 BCE (like Moses, the exact date of his life is not known), Zoroaster preached the following basic concepts. See if they sound familiar: God-Satan, Good-Evil, Light-Darkness, Angels-Demons, Death-Judgment, Heaven-Hell, and at the end of time, Resurrection of the Body and Life Everlasting. He also preached that, "There is a long period of punishment for the wicked and reward for the pious, *but thereafter, eternal joy shall reign forever (emphasis added)*." In other words, Hell is for rehabilitation, not for torture.

This idea may be as old as Zoroaster, but it is as new as modern-day near-death experiencers, some of whom died into Hell but found themselves rescued when they called out to God or Jesus.

In Judaism, Universalism is reflected in the Messianic Time described primarily in the Book of Isaiah (Is 2:2 & 4, 12:1-2, 25:6-8, 39:3, 5, 66:18 & 23, Jer 31:31-34). The Rabbis of the Midrash say that one can stay in Hell only one year.

In Christianity, the idea of Universalism is a very old and enduring theological position. Its major proponent in early Christianity was Origen (185-254 CE). In the nineteenth century, the Universalist Church was for a time the sixth largest denomination in the United States. In the twenty-first century, Universalism is advocated by Christians from diverse backgrounds, including some post-Vatican II Catholics and Primitive Baptists. The Biblical references which support Universal Salvation are second in number only to Good Works as the way to Salvation and the two taken together form the basis for Universal Restoration.

Other religions have Universalist hopes too. Although not in the *Koran*, it is written in the *Hadith* (the oral history of Mohammad) that, "Surely a day will come over Hell when there shall not be a human soul in it." The Bahai religion sees a continuous progression of souls toward perfection after death. In the East, Hinduism and its children—Buddhism, Sikhism, and Jainism—all allow for the potential for all to be saved. When my wife and I attended the Jade Buddha Temple a few years ago, they were singing, "We are not discouraged by the time it takes to save all the humans and all of the animals!"

When one looks at the plight of humanity through the eyes of a parent, it is easy to see that Universalism makes sense. God is infinitely nicer than the best human beings you know. God is in *all* of us, and we are *all* in God. God knows the assets and limitations of each human soul. Unlike the State Board of Pardons and Parole, God knows how to rehabilitate people.

Once upon a time before time mattered, people worshiped the Great Spirit, saw every living thing as possessing a spirit, and saw Afterlife as a Happy Hunting Ground. That sounds Universalist to me! So maybe we have come full circle. To quote Jesus in the non-canonical *Gospel of Thomas*:

Have you discovered the beginning, then, so that you are seeking the end? For where the beginning is, the end will be (G of Thos 18).

As a Universalist Christian, I look forward to the time when, as Jesus taught, God will save the "Lost Sheep" and the "Prodigal Son."

Notes

All *Bible* quotations are from the *New Century Version* and the *New Revised Standard Version*. The *New Century Version* was selected for clarity (NCV). Because of its easy readability, the *New Century Version* is especially good for long *Bible* passages. The *New Revised Standard Version* was utilized for precision (NRSV). The verses from the NCV are noted in the text. All other Bible verses are from the NRSV. When verses are cited but not quoted, only the *Bible* verse is listed since any translation can be used.

Quotations of Jesus are denoted by **bold** type. All statements in parentheses represent alternate wording, such as Wise Men (Magi) or Messiah (Christ, Anointed One) or alternate translations as they appear in the footnotes of the *New Revised Standard Version*. I am indebted to the publishers of the *New Century Version* and the *New Revised Standard Version* for their kind permissions listed on the copyright page of this book.

Permission for use of the material in this book is granted for church newsletters or similar "in-church" type user material. Users must acknowledge the copyright permissions noted in the front of this book and comply accordingly.

Primary Sources

1. Whole Book: Holy Bible(NCV,1996;NRSV, 1989), Brownrigg (1971), Comay (1971), Metzger (1991), Throckmorton (1960).

2. The primary references for Universal Salvation (other than the New Testament) include: Allen & Eddy (1894), Ballou (1959), Barclay, (1975), Bonda (1998), Bruce (2001), Christian (1936), Chauncy (1784/1969), Daley (1991), Dorgan (1997), Guild (1853), Gulley & Mulholland (2003), Hanson (1888), Hart (1992), Hick (1976, 1993, 1999), Hick et al (1995), Howe (1993), Klassen (2001), Linn, Linn, & Linn (1994), Ludlow (2000), Origen (1885/1994), Owen-Towle (1993), Robinson (1968), Sachs (1991), Sanders (1992), Silloway (1934), Smith (1992), Sutherland (1906), Talbott (1997), Vincent (1999, 2000, 2003), Von Balthasar (1988), Whittemore (1840/2003), and Williams (1971).

3. The primary references (other than the *New Testament*) for Salvation via Good Works include Ehrman (1999), Griffiths (1991), Klassen (2001), Koester (1996), Masumian (1995), Sim (1996), Vincent (1999, 2000), Von Balthasar (1988), and Yinger (1999).

4. The reference to John 14:6 relating to the teachings of Jesus comes from Harpur (1986) and Hick (1993). Marcus Borg (2001) has a similar view.

5. The primary source for Jesus as the only way to Salvation ("Jesus Saves") comes from religion courses I took as a freshman at Baylor University in 1961-62. The arguments and counter-arguments are also examined by the above-named theologians listed in reference notes #2 and #3. Finally, an article in *Christianity Today* by George (1997) motivated me to search for *New Testament* verses that support the various paths to salvation, including Good Works and Universal Salvation. The article made a case for "Jesus Saves" by using 23 verses from the *New Testament*; in my own review of the *New Testament*, I found 139 verses which imply "Jesus Saves". Hastings et al (1953) lists 77 verses that imply salvation by predestination.

6. The primary references for the developmental nature of religion (see Chapters 2, 3, &4) are: Argyle (2000), Fowler (1981), Hood (1995), Hood et al (1996), Vincent (2001), James (1901/1968), Ligon (1931/1961), Starbuck (1899), Wulff (1997).

7. The references to mystical religious experiences, near-death experiences, death-bed visions, and post-death visions (including visions of Hell) are Argyle (2000), Armstrong (1976), Atwater (1992), Beardsworth (1977), Bennett (1990), Borchert (1994), Borg (1997), Bucke (1901/1931), Bush (2002), Cardena (2000), Coxhead (1985), De Benniville (1782/2005) Deikman (2000), Fox (2003), Glock & Stark (1965) Greeley (1974), Greyson (2000), Greyson & Bush (1992), Hardy (1979/1997) Harpur (1991), Hay (1987, 1994), Hick (1993, 1999, 2003), Hood (1995, 2001), Hood et al (1996), Hurtado (2000), Hyslop (1908) James (1901/1958), Johnson (1998), Kalish & Rynolds (1973), Kircher (1995), Kokoszka (2000), Lead(e) (1694/2005), Levy (1937), Masumain (1995), Mitofsky Intl. & Edison Media Research (2002/2005), Newberg et al (2001), Osis & Harldsson (1977), Oxman et al (1988), Ring & Valarino (1998), Ritchie & Sherrill (1978), Rommer (2000), Rosenblatt et al (1991), Siglug (1986), Smith (1903), Stifer et al (1993), Tamminen (1994), Underhill (1911/1999,1914/1942), Vincent (1994, 2003), Wiebe (1997), Wood (1989), Wulff (1997), and Zaleski (1987).

8. The near-death cases in Chapter 8 are from Vincent (1994), Ring & Valarino (1998, p 167), Rommer (2000, p 42), and Greyson & Bush (1992, p 100).

9. A description of the references used in constructing *Appendix A* are listed in the note #3.

10. The references used in constructing *Appendices B &C* are listed in note #2.

11. The references for *Appendix G*, "Christian Universalism 'Endorsed by the Jesus "Seminar" are *Appendices A, B, & C*, the notes above in #5, and Funk, Hoover, and The Jesus Seminar (1993).

12. The references for *Appendix H*, "Magic, Deeds, and Universalism" are *Appendices A, B, & C*, the notes above in #5, and the following: Bialik & Ravnitzky (1992), Borchert (1994), Ellwood (2001), Flotz (2004), Griffiths

(1991), Hick (1976, 1993, 1999), Masumain (1995), Nigosian (2000), Teisar (1988), Underhill (1911/1991), Wilson (1995).

References

Allen, J. H. & Eddy, R. (1894) *A History of the Unitarians and the Universalists in the United States*. New York: The Christian Literature Co.

Argyle, M. (2000) *Psychology and Religion*. New York: Routledge.

Armstrong, C. J. R. (1976) *Evelyn Underhill, 1875-1941: An Introduction to Her Life and Writings*. Grand Rapids, MI: Eerdmans Publishing Co.

Atwater, P. M. H. (1992). Is there a Hell? Surprising Observations About the Near-Death Experience. *Journal of Near-Death Studies*, 10 (3), 149-160.

Ballou, H. (1959) *A Treatise on Atonement, 15th ed*. Boston: Universalist Publishing House.

Barclay, W. (1975) *A Spiritual Autobiography*. Grand Rapids, MI: Wm. B. Eerdmans Publishing Co.

Beardsworth, T. (1977) *A Sense of Presence, The Phenomenology of Certain Kinds of Visionary and Ecstatic Experience, Based on a Thousand Contemporary First-Hand Accounts*. Oxford: The Religious Experience Research Unit.

Bennett, B.M. (1990) *An Anatomy of Revelation: Prophetic Visions in the Light of Scientific Research*. Harrisburg, PA: Morehouse Publishing.

Bialik, H. N. & Ravnitzky, Y. H. (1992) *The Book of Legends: Legends from the Talmud and Midrash*, New York: Schoken Books.

Bonda, J. (1998) *The One Purpose of God*. Grand Rapids, MI: Eerdmans Publishing Co.

Borchert, B. (1994) *Mysticism*. York Beach, ME: Samuel Weiser, Inc.

Borg, M. (1997). *The God We Never Knew: Beyond Dogmatic Religion to a More Authentic Contemporary Faith*. San Francisco, CA: HarperSanFrancisco

Borg, M. (2001) *Reading the Bible Again for the First Time*. San Francisco: Harper San Francisco.

Brownrigg, R. (1971) *Who's Who In the New Testament*. NY: Holt, Rinehart, & Winston.

Bruce, C. (2001) "The Quaker and Universalist Connection" *Universalist Herald*, 153(1).

Bucke, R. M. (1901/1931) *Cosmic Consciousness*. New York; E. F. Dutton.

Budge, E. A. W. (Trans.) *Book of the Bee*. Retrieved 7/08/05 from: www.sacredtexts.com/chr/bb/bb60.htm

Bush, N. E. (2002) "Afterward: Making Meaning After a Frightening Near-Death Experience" *Journal of Near-Death Studies*, 21 (2), 99-133.

Cardena, E., Lynn, S. J., and Krippner, S. (2000*) Varieties of Anomalous Experience*. Washington, D.C.: American Psychological Association.

Christian, S. (1936) "When Christendom Was Universalist" *The Christian Leader*, 39, 902-904.

Chauncy, C. (1784/1969) *The Mystery Hid from Ages and Generations*. New York: Arno Press & The New York Times.

Comay, J.(1971) *Who's Who in the Old Testament*. NY: Holt, Rinehart & Winston.

Coxhead, N. (1985) *The Relevance of Bliss*. New York: St. Martin's Press.

Dailey, B.E. (1991) *The Hope of the Early Church*. New York: Cambridge University Press.

De Benneville, G. (1782) *The Life and Trance of George De Benneville*. Retrieved 7/08/05 from: www.uuchristian.net/uuchristian.org/eu/lifetran.htm

Deikman, A. J. (2000) "A Functional Approach to Mysticism" *Journal of Consciousness Studies*, 7, 11-12, 75-91.

Dorgan, H. (1997) *In the Hands of a Happy God: The "No-Hellers" of Central Appalachia*. Knoxville, TN: University of Tennessee Press.

Dunn, J. D. G. (1975/1997). *Jesus and the Spirit: A Study of the Religious and Charismatic Experience of Jesus and the First Christians as Reflected in the New Testament*. Grand Rapids, MI: William B. Eerdmans.

Ehrman, B.D. (1999) *Jesus, Apocalyptic Prophet of the New Millennium*. NY: Oxford.

Ellwod, G. F. (2001) *The Uttermost Deep: The Challenge of Near-Death Experiences*, NY: Lantern Books.

Flotz, R. C. (2004) *Spirituality in the Land of the Noble*, Oxford: Oneworld.

Fowler, J.W. (1981) *Stages of Faith*. San Francisco: Harper & Row.

Fox, M. (2003) *Religion, Spirituality, and the Near-Death Experience*. New York: Routhledge.

Funk, R. W., Hoover, R. W. and The Jesus Seminar. (1993). *The Five Gospels, The Search for the Authentic Words of Jesus*. New York: Macmillian Publishing Co.

Funk, RW., and The Jesus Seminar. (1998). *The Acts of Jesus: The Search for the Authentic Deeds of Jesus*. San Francisco, CA: HarperSanFracisco.

George, T. (1997) "The Gift of Salvation" *Christianity Today*, Dec. 8, 35-37.

Glock, C. Y, and Stark, R (1965). *Religion and Society in Tension*. Chicago, IL: Rand McNally.

Greeley, A.M. (1974) *Ecstasy*. Englewood Cliffs, NJ: Prentice-Hall, Inc.

Greyson, B. & Bush, N.E. (1992) "Distressing Near Death Experiences" *Psychiatry*, 55, 95-110.

Greyson, B. (2000). Near-Death Experiences. In Cardella, E., Lynn, S. J., and Krippner, S. (eds.), *Varieties of Anomalous Experience: Examining the Scientific Evidence*. Washington, DC: American Psychological Association.

Griffiths, J.G. (1991) *The Divine Verdict*. New York: Brill.

Guild, E. E. (1853) *Universalists Book of Reference*. Retrieved 2-3-03 from: www.tentmaker.org/books/InfavorCh.20.html

Gulley, P. & Mulholland, J. (2003) *If Grace Is True: Why God Will Save Every Person*. San Francisco: HarperSanFancisco.

Hanson, J.W. (1877/2003) *Bible Proofs of Universal Salvation*. Whitefish, MT: Kessinger Publishing.

Hardy, A. (1979/1997) *The Spiritual Nature of Man*. Oxford: The Religious Experience Research Centre.

Harpur, T. (1986) *For Christ's Sake*. Toronto: McClelland & Stewart.

Harpur, T. (1991) *Life After Death*. Toronto: McClelland & Stewart.

Hart, T. (1992) "Universalism: Two Distinct Types." In, de S. Cameron, N.M. (Ed.), *Universalism and the Doctrine of Hell*. Grand Rapids, MI: Baker Book House.

Hastings, J., Grant, F.C., & Rowley, H.H. (Eds.) (1953*) Dictionary of the Bible*. N.Y.: Charles Scribner's Sons.

Hay, D. (1987) *Exploring Inner Space: Scientists and Religious Experience*. London: Mowbray.

Hay, D. (1994) "The Biology of God": What is the Current status of Hardy's Hypothesis? *The International Journal for the Psychology of Religion*, 4 (1), 1-23.

Hick, J. (1976) *Death and Eternal Life*. New York: Harper & Row.

Hick, J. (1993a) *Disputed Questions In Theology and the Philosophy of Religion*. New Haven, CN: Yale University Press.

Hick, J. (1993b). *The Metaphor of God Incarnate: Christology in a Pluralistic Age*. Louisville, KY: Westminster/John Knox Press.

Hick, J. (1999) *The Fifth Dimension*. Boston: One World.

Hick, J. (2003) *John Hick: An Autobiography*. Oxford: Oneworld Publications.

Hick, J., Pinnock, C.H., McGarth, A.E., Geivett, R.D., & Phillips, W.G. (1995) *More Than One Way?* Grand Rapids, MI: Zondervan Publishing House.

Holy Bible, New Century Version (The Everyday Study Bible) (NCV). (1996) Dallas: World Bibles.

Holy Bible, New Revised Standard Version (NRSV). (1989) Nashville: Thomas Nelson.

Hood, R.W. (1995) *Handbook of Religious Experience.* Birmingham, Al: Religious Education Press.

Hood, R.W. (2001) *Dimensions of Mystical Experiences: Empirical Studies and Psychological Links.* New York: Rodopi.

Hood, R.W., Spilka, B., Hunsberger, B. & Gorsuch, R. (1996) *The Psychology of Religion, 2nd Ed.* NY: Guilford Press.

Howe, C. A. (1993) *The Larger Faith: A Short History of American Universalism.* Boston: Skinner House Books.

Hurtado, L.W. (2000) "Religious Experience and Religious Innovation in the New Testament" *Journal of Religion,* 80 (2), 183-205.

Hyslop. J. H. (1908) *Psychical Research and the Resurrection.* Boston: Small, Maynard, and Co.

James, W. (1901/1958) *Varieties of Religious Experience.* New York: Signet

Johnson, L. T. (1998). *Religious Experience in Earliest Christianity: A Missing Dimension in New Testament Studies.* Minneapolis, MN: Fortress Press.

Kalish, R.A. & Rynolds, D.K. (1973) "Phenomenological Reality and Post-Death Contact" *Journal for the Scientific Study of Religion,* 12 (2), 209-221.

Kircher, P.M. (1995) *Love Is the Link.* Burdett, NY: Larson Publications.

Klassen, R.J. (2001) *What Does the Bible Really Say About Hell?* Telford, PA: Pandora Press U.S.

Koester, H. (1996) "The Second Coming Demythologized" *Bible Review,* Vol. 12 (5).

Kokoszka, A. (2000) Altered States of Consciousnessw; A Comparison of Profoundly and Superficially Altered States. *Imagination, Cognition and Personality*, 19 (2), 165-184.

Lead(e), J. (1694) *The Enochian Walks with God.* Retrived 7/08/05 from: www.sigler.org/shofar/janeleade/enochian.htm

Levy, H. (1937) Why Believe in God? *The Christian Leader*, 120 (13), 396-398.

Ligon, E. M. (1936/1961) *The Psychology of Christian Personality.* New York: Macmillan Co.

Linn, D., Linn, S.F., & Linn, M. (1994) *Good Goats.* New York: Paulist Press.

Ludlow, M. (2000) *Universal Salvation: Eschatology In the Thought of Gregory of Nissa and Karl Rahner.* New York: Oxford University Press.

Masumian, F. (1995) *Life After Death.* Oxford: One World.

Metzger, B.M. (1991) *NRSV Exhaustive Concordance.* Nashville, TN: Thomas Nelson Publishers.

Mitofsky International and Edison Media Research. (2002). Exploring religious America. *Religion & Ethics Newsweekly*, May 10, 2002, Retrieved May 16, 2002, from: www.pbs.org/wnet/religionandethics/week534/cover.html

Newberg, A., D'Aquili, E., & Rause, V. (2001*) Why God Won't Go Away: Brain Science and the Biology of Belief.* NY: Ballantine Books.

Nigosian, S. A. (2000) *World Religions (3rd Ed.)* New York: Bedford/St. Martins.

Origen in Roberts, A.R. & Donaldson, J. (Eds.)(1885/1994) *Ante-Nicene Fathers, Vol.4&10.* Grand Rapids, MI: Wm. B. Eerdmans Publishing Co.

Osis, K. & Haraldsson, E. (1977) *At the Hour of Death.* NY: Avon Books.

Owen-Towle, T. (1993) *The Gospel of Universalism.* Boston: Skinner House Books.

Oxman, T.E. et al (1988) "The Language of Altered States" *Journal of Nervous and Mental Disease*, 176 (7), 401-408.

Ring, K., and Valarino, E. E. (1998). *Lessons from the Light: What We Can Learn from the Near-Death Experience*. New York, NY: Plenum/Insight.

Ritchie, G. G., and Sherrill, E. (1978). *Return from Tomorrow*. Old Tappan, NJ: Sprite.

Robinson, J. A. T. (1968) *In the End God*. New York: Harper & Row.

Rommer, B.R. (2000) *Blessing In Disguise*. St.Paul, MN: Llewellyn.

Rosenblatt, P.C., Meyer, C.J. & Karis, T. (1991) "Internal interactions with God" *Imagination, Cognition, and Personality*, 11 (1), 85-97.

Sachs, J.R. (1991) "Current Eschatology: Universal Salvation and the Problem of Hell" *Theological Studies*, 52, 227-254.

Sanders, J. (1992) *No Other Name*. Grand Rapids, MI: Wm. Eerdmens Pub. Co.

Siglug, M.A. (1986) *Schizophrenic and Mystical Experiences: Similarities and Differences*. Unpublished Doctoral Dissertation, University of Detroit.

Silloway, P.M. (1934) "Universalism in Parable" *The Christian Leader*, 117 (51), 1612-1614.

Sim, D.C. (1996) *Apocalyptic Eschatology in the Gospel of Matthew*. Cambridge: Cambridge University Press.

Smith, J.D. (1992) *The Ancient Wisdom of Origen*. London: Associated University Press.

Smith, H. W. (1903) *The Unselfishness of God and How I Discovered it: A Spiritual Autobiography*. New York: Fleming & Revel Co.

Smith, J.I. & Haddad, Y. Y. (1981) The Islamic Understanding of Death and Resurrection, Albany, NY: State University of New York Press.

Stifler, K., Greer, J., Sneck, W., and Douenmuehle, R. (1993) "An Empirical Investigation of the Discriminability of Reported Mystical Experiences Among Religious Contemplatives, Psychotic Inpatients, and Normal Adults" *Journal for the Scientific Study of Religion*. 32 (4), 366-372.

Starbuck, E. D. (1899) *The Psychology of Religion*. New York: Charles Scribner's Sons.

Sutherland, J.T. (1906) *Some Leading Points of Unitarian Belief*. In Melton, J. G. (1991) *American Religious Creeds*, Vol. III. New York: Triumph Press.

Talbott, T. (1997) *The Inescapable Love of God*. Parkland, FL: Universal Publishers.

Tamminen, K. (1994) Religious Experiences in Childhood and Adolescence: A Viewpoint of Religious Development Between Ages 7 and 20. *The International Journal of the Psychology of Religion*, 4 (2), 61-85.

Teiser, S. F. (1988) *The Ghost Festival in Medieval China*, Princeton, NJ: Princeton University Press.

Throckmorton, B.H. (Ed.) (1960) *Gospel Parallels*. Nashville, TN: Thomas Nelson, Inc.

Underhill, E. (1911/1999) *Mysticism*. Oxford: Oneworld Publications.

Underhill, E. (1914/1942) *Practical Mysticism*. Columbus, OH: Ariel Press.

Vincent, K.R. (1994) *Visions of God from the Near Death Experience*. Burdett, New York: Larson Publications.

Vincent, K.R. (1999) *THE MAGI: From Zoroaster to the "Three Wise Men"*. North Richland Hills, TX: Bibal Press.

Vincent, K.R. (2000) "Unitarian and Universalist Concepts of Salvation in the Bible and World Religion" *Universalist Herald*, 152 (5).

Vincent, K.R. (2001) "Developmental Revelation" *Universalist Herald*, 153 (5).

Vincent, K.R. (2003) "The Near-Death Experience and Christian Universalism" *Journal of Near-Death Studies*, 22 (1), 57-71.

Von Balthasar, H.U. (1988) *Dare We Hope That All Men Be Saved?* San Francisco: Ignatius Press.

Whittemore, T. (1840) *100 Scriptural Proofs that Jesus Christ will Save All Mankind*. Retrieved 1-31-03 from: www.tentmaker.org/books/ScriptualProofs.html

Wiebe, D.H. (1997) *Visions of Jesus*. New York: Oxford University Press.

Williams, G. H. (1971) "American Universalism" *Journal of the Universalist Historical Society*, 9.

Wilson, A. (Ed.) (1995) *World Scripture*, St. Paul, MN: Paragon House.

Wood, F. W. (1989) *An American Profile—Opinions and Behavior 1972-1989*. Chicago: National Opinion Research Center.

Wulff, D.M. (1997) *Psychology of Religion, 2nd Ed*. NY: John Wiley & Sons.

Yinger, K. L. (1999) *Paul, Judaism, and Judgment According to Deeds*. Cambridge University Press.

Zaleski, C. (1987). *Otherworld Journeys: Accounts of Near-Death Experience in Medieval and Modern Times*. New York, NY: Oxford University Press.

978-0-595-36683-5
0-595-36683-X

Printed in the United States
44930LVS00010B/75